A Christian Considers Divorce and Remarriage

E. Earl Joiner

A Christian Considers DIVORCE

and Remarriage

BROADMAN PRESS
Nashville, Tennessee

Unless otherwise noted, all Scripture quotations are from the King James Version of the Bible.

Scripture quotations marked (NASB) are from the *New American Standard Bible*. Copyright © The Lockman Foundation, 1960, 1962, 1963, 1968, 1971, 1972, 1973, 1975, 1977. Used by permission.

Scripture quotations marked (NIV) are from the HOLY BIBLE *New International Version*, copyright © 1978, New York Bible Society. Used by permission.

Scripture quotations marked (RSV) are from the Revised Standard Version of the Bible, copyrighted 1946, 1952, © 1971, 1973.

To
the **divorcees**
from whom
I have learned much
and
to my wife, **Geraldine,**
who did not divorce me
while I wrote this book

Acknowledgments

I am very grateful to Dean Robert S. Chauvin, President Pope A. Duncan, and my colleagues in the Department of Religion at Stetson University who have given me encouragement and support in my writing ventures. I am particularly thankful to my secretary, Mrs. Lillian Hallis, who patiently typed this manuscript in the midst of many other duties.

I am also indebted to a number of authors from whom I have borrowed directly and others who have influenced my perspective in ways that are difficult to document. I have tried to be faithful in giving proper credit, but I may have failed to do justice to my feelings of appreciation of what I have learned from many writers. In fact one of my first thoughts in beginning this work and discovering so many good books already written on the subject of divorce was: why write another one. My only defense is that I hope I have produced something that is unique and deserves to have a place among the other good books on divorce and remarriage.

Introduction

Some years ago friends of mine were coming home from a social function where they had learned to their surprise that two couples who were mutual friends of theirs were getting a divorce. As they expressed their concern, the wife slowly became introspective and wondered if the divorce disease were catching. Then without warning she turned to her husband and asked, "John, have you ever considered leaving me?"

Without a moment's hesitation, John answered, "No, never."

"Are you sure," she asked, perhaps giving expression to some self-doubt, as well as the feeling of uncertainty about the relationship that sometimes comes to many if not most couples.

John replied, "Absolutely sure." Then he added in a lighter vein than his wife had shown, "Of course I have considered killing you a time or two, but divorce never."

John was not serious, of course, or was he? So far as I know they are still living together. What John was saying, however, is more important as an illustration than it is as an indication of the state of his marriage. What John was saying reminds me of what I consider to be a fact, namely, that many people get divorced who never thought it would happen to them. They may consider other things, but not that. Many of those do not consider it seriously and still wind up getting one. They do so because the number of frustrations in the marriage multiply until one day one partner decides, "This is it! I can't stand any more," and walks out. Often the precipitating factor in the decision to leave was not a very significant disagreement and, therefore, not a real cause of the breakup. Either of the partners may have considered killing the other but got a divorce instead. That *is* the lesser of two evils.

Being the lesser of two evils brings little consolation. No matter how you look at it, divorce is a painful, often destructive process. Being a Christian doesn't immunize people from divorce or the pain that comes with it. In fact, for Christians there is a dimension that may heighten the pain of divorce. Not only is divorce a painful experience for the partners in the breakup of a marriage but it is painful for other members of the family as well. Often it is a shock to the parents of both partners. It is generally traumatic for children of the divorced parents, regardless of their ages. It seems especially difficult for small children. It is also painful for the friends of those whose marriage is breaking up. Often friends of the newly divorced do not know how to respond to the tragedy and sometimes increase the pain of the divorce by making no response at all. Finally, it is painful for the pastor who feels called to minister to family life in general and to each individual in the family.

In my thirty-five years as a Christian minister, I have had to wrestle with what the Christian's attitude toward divorce and remarriage should be. For me, this hasn't been an academic exercise. In my first pastorate of a mission while a college student, I had to face these issues. The clerk of the mission where I served as pastor had been divorced by her husband some years earlier. She later remarried and someone suggested to her that she was living in adultery. She wrote to ask what I thought. I replied that I did not think she was living in adultery, but I confess that at the time I did not feel at all confident of the validity of my answer. The inquiry drove me to reflection on the problem, and I vowed to give some serious study to the problem. For the past several years, I have been in the process of studying the problem as I have engaged in two activities. First, I have for several years now conducted a conference on Divorce and Remarriage at retreats for adult singles at Lake Yale, a retreat center sponsored by the Sunday School Department of the Florida Baptist Convention. The responses I have received from hundreds of divorcees attending these conferences has inspired the efforts involved in this venture. Second, I have been often involved, and am involved presently, in counseling with those considering divorce and with those who have been divorced.

I have written this book with several types of readers in mind. First, I have written for those married persons whose marriage is in the process of breaking up. Faced with this situation, persons ask, How can this happen to me? Is it right to get a divorce? If you are in this situation, you may want to begin with chapter 3, "Considering Getting a Divorce." This chapter contains some questions and considerations that anyone considering divorce should deal with. You will also want to read chapters 1 and 2. These chapters reexamine biblical teachings which are relevant to the issues of divorce and remarriage. Also, should you decide to get a divorce, you may need to read chapter 4, "Problems in the Process of Divorce: Legal, Moral, Spiritual."

Second, I have written for divorcees. From my experience, I have found that many divorcees struggle with uncertainty and despair as they face social ostracism by former friends. Many carry heavy loads of guilt and wonder if they are now second-class citizens. Often the friends of divorcees and even their pastors contribute to the heavy burdens they carry. If you are a divorcee, you may want to begin with chapters 5 and 6. You will also want to look at the reexamination of biblical teachings on divorce in chapters 1 and 2. If you have children you may want to read chapter 8, "Helping the Children to Adjust," because divorce is harder on children than many people imagine. If after reading these chapters you wish to consider remarriage, chapter 7, "Whether or Not to Remarry: The Hazards and Possibilities," might be helpful to you.

Third, I have written for pastors and other counselors of divorcees and those considering divorce. Having struggled with these issues myself for nearly four decades, I am particularly sympathetic to pastors who have honestly understood the teaching of Jesus as condemning remarriage for the divorcee, except in case of adultery. I have known pastors who experienced conflict within themselves because on the one hand they interpreted Jesus' teaching as I have described. On the other hand, they felt genuine compassion for the divorcee and wanted to be helpful and did not know how to do so. Pastors may want to begin with chapters 1 and 2. They may then want to look at appendixes A and B. Appendix A is a look at the social context in which we find ourselves and how divorce is related to a number of social factors. Also, you may want to look at Appendix B which looks at attitudes of the church toward divorce over the past 1900 years. In addition, pastors may want to read chapter 3, "Considering Getting a Divorce," because often those persons in the church who consider getting a divorce will seek counsel from their minister before doing so. Some of the same factors that are important to the married persons considering getting a divorce may be helpful for a counselor to consider.

Fourth, I have written the book for church members and church leaders who are concerned about whether persons who have been divorced should be given certain responsibilities within the church for which they are qualified.

Finally, I have written the book for friends of divorcees who feel a genuine need and desire to understand the difficulties of the divorcees. A basic reason for the importance of these friends is that many, perhaps most, divorcees will never go to a professional counselor but will rely only on counsel they receive from friends. For example, many of my own friends who are not divorced and who are not ministers or counselors have expressed keen interest in the book because they want to learn how to be most helpful to their friends who are considering divorce or who are going through the process of adjustment after divorce. Many of these friends may want to begin with Appendix A which should help them to understand the divorce problem in our society. You may also want to read Appendix B which deals with divorce in Christian history. You then may either wish to read the other chapters straight through, or you may wish to concentrate on those chapters which relate most specifically to the specific situation of your friends.

Contents

1
Divorce and Remarriage in the Old Testament

While Christians usually view the Old Testament by the light they receive from the New Testament in general and from the teachings of Jesus in particular, it is helpful to view the teachings of the Old Testament on divorce and remarriage in the context of ancient Israel as well. The reason is that those who wrote the New Testament were profoundly influenced by the Old Testament. Therefore, the Old Testament can give us considerable help in understanding the teachings of the New Testament.

The Place of Woman in the Old Testament

Many discussions of divorce in the Bible suffer from the failure of the writer to relate the direct and indirect references to divorce to the position of woman in relation to man in the Old Testament as a whole. It is true that most writers on divorce take note of the authority position of man and the dependency of woman.[1] They even observe that woman had some freedom. However, they fail to document sufficiently the tension between male dominance and female dependency and the paradoxical assertions which may point to stress on the equality of the sexes in some early periods of Hebrew history and to the loss of that equality during a later period. These paradoxical assertions may also reflect the awareness among some leaders of ancient Israel of a need to restore to woman her proper dignity as a person before God. I think a proper appraisal of Old Testament teaching on divorce must be set in the context of the position of woman as a whole in relation to man.

Despite the argument about a neglected element, the first point to be made is that the dominant viewpoint in the Old Testament is that woman is subject to man. This viewpoint was one the Hebrews shared with many of their ancient neighbors in the Mediterranean world.[2] This view may have been expressed in the popular but erroneous understanding of the origin of the word *woman*. Baab says that the term *woman* came from a different root from the term *man*. The similarity of the words for *man* and *woman* in Hebrew has confused that fact. The term commonly translated *man* or *male* in the Old Testament is *Ish*, and the term commonly translated *woman* is *Ashah*. Although the words look similar in both Hebrew and English, the origin of both words appears uncertain. However, there is some agreement that the two words do not come from the same root. One possible root for *Ish* is an Assyrian word *isanu* which means strong. This might suggest a contrast with woman who was regarded as weak. A more likely root for the word *Ish*, man, is *anasu*, which means to be weak, or sick. The word *woman* may have come from the word *anash*, which means soft or delicate. In short, the notion that woman is inferior or subordinate because Genesis 2:23 says she was taken out of man is not justified by this Genesis statement or the etymology of the words for man and woman.[3] However, it seems possible that cultural developments resulted in the imposing of differences between man and woman that were not originally intended.

Phyllis Tribble and others have provided some needed corrective to traditional understandings of man-woman relationships in the Old Testament. She says, for example, that Genesis 2:7 to 3:24 suggests male superiority and female inferiority as the will of God. Woman is presented as a troublemaker and as a source of temptation and man is given the right to rule over her. She argues, however, that although these passages are seen as supporting male superiority, such use violates the intent of the passage, which among other things, is to show that woman, rather than being weak, is in fact the climax of creation, the fulfillment of humanity in sexuality.[4] However, they also finally affirm the tragedy of the estrangement of man and woman from each other and from God.[5] Tribble adds that the Song of Songs presents a picture of the male-female relationships as overcome,[6] and she interprets the Book of Ruth as the story of women working out their own relationships with men in a man's world.[7]

Although the earliest records of women gave them high status in society in some areas of the ancient Near East, by the time of the Hebrews came on the scene, they were losing status rapidly and were widely subjected to man's authority as property.[8] The wide acceptance of this view of woman as subordinate to man is further illustrated in other references in the Old Testament. One example is the fact that a wife is sometimes mentioned as belonging to a man. Saul gave David's wife to another man; but since David never divorced Michal, he assumed the right to demand that she be returned to him; and she was (2 Sam. 3:13-16). Here the rights over the woman were transferred three times, while the woman we assume had no voice in any of these decisions. Another example, to receive attention later, is the fact that the initiative to get a divorce was given to the man alone (Deut. 24:1-3). A woman might get a divorce, but only if the man initiated it.

The second observation we can make about woman in the Old Testament is that, in their theological position before God, in social and in economic life, military and family life, woman and man often appear as equals. Often these suggestions of equality are overlooked by biblical scholars. For example, Baab in *The Interpreter's Dictionary of the Bible* cites Genesis 2:24-25 and 3:8 as support for his contention that among the Hebrews woman belonged to man.[9] While we have observed the subjection of woman to man, we must point out here that to use the fact that the woman (Eve) is referred to as "his wife," (Adam) states only one side of the situation. Baab fails to note that in Genesis 3:7 Adam is referred to as "her husband." Here the subjection is mutual. There is a parallel further in Genesis 1, where man and woman appear on an equal basis. Further, in the story of the fall, while Eve ate the forbidden fruit first, when called to account by God, Adam first shifted the blame for his own disobedience. That is, both sinned equally. Furthermore Phyllis Tribble points out that although the Bible prefers male metaphors, both male and female imagery are used in describing God.[10] This suggests that the theology of ancient Israel reflected a feminine as well as a masculine perspective.

Their religious equality is seen not only in that woman shared in many of the religious festivals of ancient Israel (Ex. 15:20, Deut. 16:14, Judg. 21:19-21) but also demonstrated religious sensitivity and insight that was recognized, however reluctantly, by the male religious leadership of ancient Israel. A classic example is the picture of Miriam in Exodus. There she appears as a prophetess who considered herself as equal to Moses (Ex. 15:20 *ff.*). Her condemnation was not likely due to her comparison to

Moses as a prophet, but to her speaking *against* Moses for marrying an Ethiopian woman (Num. 12:1-15). In this connection, it is significant to note Moses' intercession on Miriam's behalf and her subsequent restoration to the community (Num. 12:13-15). The story of Miriam, moreover, should prepare one to observe the prominent role played by Deborah (Judg. 4—5) and later by the prophetess Huldah at a very important period of Judah's history when the reform was inaugurated during the reign of Josiah (2 Kings 22:14-20; 2 Chron. 34:22-28).

The socioeconomic prominence of women in the Old Testament is reflected in the varied roles they often shared in weddings, funerals, harvest festivals, and other social occasions. Furthermore, while such references are rare, the inclusion of the proverbs of Lemuel in the Book of Proverbs may reflect a significant advance in the thought of post-Exilic Judaism when this material was assimilated. Proverbs 31, the picture of an ideal woman, includes the description of a woman who competed on an equal basis with men in the business world. She both manufactured and marketed economic goods.

The prominence of women in political and military life is uncommon among the ancient Hebrews, but the few examples that appear are significant. Some of them are presented as normal and accepted facts. Among them are the story of Deborah (Judg. 5), Bathsheba (1 Kings 1:11 *ff.*), Jezebel (1 Kings 19:1 *ff.*), and Athaliah (2 Kings 11:1 *ff.*). The notoriety of Jezebel and Athaliah does not contradict the fact that their influence as women was accepted. Their condemnation in the Old Testament is due to their evil ways, not to their sex.

Women also played a significant role in the arts of ancient Israel.[11] Miriam was apparently the leader of a group of women who danced and sang in celebration of the departure of the Hebrews from Egypt (Ex. 15:20). Later "singing women" and "singing men" appear to have played an equal role in the Temple worship system (1 Chron. 35:25; Neh. 7:67). Samuel Terrien says that the change in the religious status among the Hebrews may have resulted from the reaction of the Hebrews to the mother goddess cult of the Canaanites.[12] Both the subordination and the concern for equality are reflected in the teaching on divorce found in Deuteronomy.

In summary, it appears that, while the subordination of woman to man is dominant in the Old Testament, there is also some ambivalence in the relation of man and woman. It appears probable that, in early Hebrew history, religious equality between the sexes was more common, but by the post-Exilic period, woman had lost most of her status in the religious system.

Male Initiative

The first thing that strikes one in Deuteronomy is that the privilege and initiative for obtaining a divorce is given to the man alone. There is not the slightest hint anywhere that the woman might initiate divorce proceedings. This fact reflects the position of woman among the ancient Hebrews, particularly during and following the Exile. The only apparent exception to this rule I have found is in the Elephantine Papyri, dating around the fifth century BC.

These papyri were left by a community of Hebrews who lived on Elephantine Island in the Nile River during the time when Persia ruled both Palestine and Egypt. The papyri consist largely of legal documents. Among them there is a deed dating around 459 BC, concerning the reversion of property. Part of that deed reads, "If tomorrow or some other day you build upon this land, and then my daughter divorces you and leaves you, you shall have no power to take it or give it to others."[13] This deed seems to imply that in this colony a wife was permitted to seek a divorce. But the absence of such a custom from later Jewish literature and from Jewish tradition today suggests that it was a departure from mainline Hebrew thought and reflected the influence of foreign cultures.

However, one should not assume that the restriction of woman's freedom and right on this subject represents the whole story in the Old Testament on woman in relation to man. It appears that at the dawn of Hebrew history the place of woman in relation to man was subordinate; indeed she was the property of man. In time the social consciousness and sense of responsibility reflected in the laws of the Old Testament, especially in Deuteronomy, brought changes in Hebrew thought. Woman continued to be regarded as subject to man, but a growing sense of responsibility and respect for her rights is seen in numerous places, including the divorce law itself. The beautiful tribute to a virtuous woman in Proverbs, when examined with care, probably does not fit the image the average person who reads the Old Testament has of woman in Hebrew society. While most of us who are men note the work she does in the home, we may overlook the fact that this ideal woman also feels free to participate in the business and professional affairs of the world.

The divorce law of Deuteronomy 24, which places the initiative with man alone, should not be viewed as a deliberate discrimination against woman. It merely reflects the fact that man was still regarded as the protector of woman. The placing of the initiative with the man simply reminded him of his responsibility to protect his wife. Certainly it also reflects the right of a man to reject his wife if he had sufficient reason. While we shall discuss the question of sufficient reason presently, for the moment, it is important to point out that a man could not dispose of his wife for any and every reason, despite the liberal version of the law that was popular in some Hebrew circles much later.

Serious Grounds

The classic statement of the law of divorce in Deuteronomy 24:1 *ff.* is that a man may divorce his wife if "she find no favor in his eyes, because he hath found some uncleanness in her." From a study of the interpretation of this passage in later Judaism, two things seem clear. First, there has been disagreement almost from the time this law was written to the present as to its intended meaning. In the time of Jesus, for example, one group of rabbis followed Hillel who focused on the first part of the statement about the wife finding "no favor" in the husband's eyes. Thus, Hillel taught that a man could divorce his wife if she displeased him in any way. This interpretation places stress on the subjective element in the husband. Here, there is no objective standard by which anyone might judge the validity of the husband's decision. A second rabbi, Shammai, placed stress on the *reason* for a woman losing favor. According to Shammai, there must be a good reason—a generally recognized serious offense—for a man to divorce his wife. He linked the loss of "favor" and the reason and, thus, appears to have stressed a standard for the decision which is more objective. The reason stated in the divorce law is "some uncleanness" or "indecency" in her. The word *ervah,* used here, literally means nudity and as sometimes used in the Old Testament is connected with sex, including illegitimate sex. One may debate the propriety of separating the loss of favor and the indecency the way the schools of Shammai and Hillel did. However, it seems probable that these two schools came into being because of uncertainty as to how to interpret the law. It seems probable, moreover, that the dominant reason that was most widely accepted as a legitimate cause for divorce was infidelity. Therefore, despite the liberal position of Hillel, it appears that through the centuries, the prevailing opinion of Israel's moral leaders was that a man was not to divorce his wife without a good reason. Baab believes that in Matthew 1:19; 5:31-32; and 19:1-9, Jesus was merely reflecting the dominant opinion in Judaism.[14]

In my opinion, the law of Deuteronomy never intended the subjective and the objective elements in the law to be separated as they are in the two interpretations of Hillel (subjective) and Shammai (objective). This point may be implied in the fact that Jesus refused to take side in the debate between the two schools. The intention of the law was probably to stress the responsibility of the husband in a society where he had much freedom. However, although the law here recognizes that men did divorce their wives because of what they regarded as indecency, it does not require that a man divorce his wife because of indecency. It only implies that *if* she loses favor with him because of her indecency and he does reject her, he must give her a statement that he has divorced her. This is an important element in the freedom of the woman, the full significance of which will be presented shortly.

The Divorce Bill: Freedom and Dignity for the Woman

Far from merely reflecting the subjection of women which was typical of the ancient Near East, the requirement that the rejected wife be given a certificate was a great step forward for the wife. This point was first recognized by Jesus. The divorce decree required that a rejected wife be given her freedom, including the freedom to remarry. Thus, the divorce law demands the restoration of dignity and freedom for the rejected wife. The divorce law may have been a way of saying that it was a cruel thing for a man to keep a woman in subjection to him and continue to punish her by rejection because of something she did. David did this to Michal. Despite her love and the fact that she saved him from death at the hands of Saul, when she criticized David, he rejected her. This was after David insisted that Michal be returned to him after Saul gave her to someone else (cf. 1 Sam. 18:20,27-28; 19:11-17; 25:44; 2 Sam. 3:13-14; 6:16-23).

In a society where first marriages were commonly arranged by parents, it may be that a woman with a bill of divorce was the most free woman in the community. Of course, there were problems as to how she could exercise her freedom, and there were economic problems. The Old Testament gives no direct answer as to how the divorced free woman survived. We can only guess that some returned to their families, some remarried, and some drifted into prostitution out of economic desperation.

Although many Old Testament scholars distinguish between the "indecency" of Deuteronomy 24:1 and adultery which calls for the death penalty (Lev. 20:10; Deut. 22:22-24), they are neither clear nor agreed on the nature of the difference. The fact that the law calls for the death of both the man and the woman in the case of adultery calls attention to an element of equality in the law. The scanty evidence of actual executions for adultery and for executions of the law regulating divorce may suggest that neither executions nor divorce were common. Hosea, for example, appears to have divorced his wife (Hos. 2:2-3), but she does not seem to have been executed. On the contrary, because she did not remarry, he could and did remarry her in accordance with the law, which prohibited a man from remarrying the wife he divorces after she has married another (Deut. 24:4).

Although there is not enough concrete evidence to make a strong argument, it appears possible from Hosea's example and from his own stress on mercy that he had three options. One was that he might forgive her and keep her. The second was that he might invoke the law and have her tried by the community and executed by stoning. The third option was that he might send her away from his home. If he did so, he was bound to restore her to freedom and dignity by giving her a bill of divorce. Hosea chose to divorce his wife. Later he forgave her and took her back. Compared to death, that was a very humane thing to do, and it may indicate the profound sensitivity to persons even beyond that which is reflected in the Deuteronomic law.

The Practice of Divorce in the Old Testament

Very likely divorce was never common in the Old Testament. The strong emphasis on the unity of the family, the responsibility of family loyalty, the prohibition of adultery, and the psychic strength of the community all discouraged divorce. The rarity of divorce is silently attested to by the fact that concrete examples are almost completely absent in the Old Testament. Johannes Pederson says that the reason for divorcing a wife among the ancient Hebrews was generally her failure to produce children, yet he does not cite a single example.[15] It is true that the Old Testament abounds in references to the importance of childbearing (see Gen. 17—18; 29:34; 30:1; 1 Sam. 1:11), but it seems very uncertain as to whether or not the usual reason for divorce was childlessness.

We may only speculate on the grounds for divorce because we have few examples. However, while divorce was never common among the ancient Hebrews, references to divorce in the laws of Deuteronomy suggest that the practice of divorce did exist. For example, Deuteronomy 22:13-19 and 22:23-28 define two examples in which divorce was absolutely prohibited. In those situations, one should not put away his wife. The first was where the husband accused his wife of not being a virgin and he was proved wrong. The second was where a man was forced to marry his wife because he raped her. The existence of these laws in Deuteronomy 22 and 24 probably resulted from the growth of the custom on divorce in the latter years of ancient Israel's history. The last reference to divorce in the Old Testament, Malachi 2:14-16, suggests that divorce was becoming more common and that God disapproved of it. Philip Sigal sees Malachi's position as a regression, a departure from the plain teachings of the law. He states that it reflected a point of view that was developing in Judaism but was not triumphant until Christianity came on the scene. Moreover, while he also mentions the opposition of Malachi to the mixed marriages which became a problem after the return from the Babylonian Exile, he fails to note the possibility that Malachi's concern may not be to set aside the teaching of the law, but to condemn the common practice of divorce at the time of Ezra. That practice was based on an old law that was then given an interpretation and application that went beyond its originally intended meaning. I refer here to the old law which forbade mixed marriages.

The original reason for the prohibition of mixed marriages was not racial, but religious, reflecting the danger of resulting lapses into idolatry and polytheism. It seems clear that by the return from the Exile, the Hebrews were largely cured of both. What Malachi may have been saying is that he was still opposed to mixed marriages because, while the danger of idolatry and polytheism was less, it was still a danger (2:10-12). However, when he went on in 2:13-16 to condemn divorce, Malachi might have been saying that God does not approve of divorce merely because of religious differences.[16] Therefore, it seems possible that while Malachi did not approve of marriages to pagans, he did not understand the law either to require or justify divorce of those who have consummated mixed marriages.

Sigal argues that Malachi is the basis of the view presented in the Gospels. We shall discuss that question later. Here I can only say that Malachi's view seems consistent with the view set forth by Jesus, but that Malachi might have not been condemning divorce as a matter of principle, but simply reiterating the responsibility of fidelity to the covenant commitment that is involved in marriage. He did imply a condemnation of divorce for minor reasons.

The Book of Ezra provides an example of a problem that was faced in different form among the Romans of the fifth century BC. The question was over the propriety and legitimacy of marriage between plebeians and patricians. Around 450 BC Pericles had legislation passed in Greece that required Athenian citizenship by both parents in order for offspring to be given citizenship.[17] Both the Greeks and the Romans became seriously concerned about maintaining the purity of their own cultural heritage and traditions. Similarly, a central concern of the returning Hebrew exiles was to preserve the purity of their religious traditions. To this end they began by researching their own records to be sure that all the exiles to return to Jerusalem were direct descendants of the original tribes of Judah and Benjamin or the priests and Levites. Those whose family records did not prove their family ancestry were excluded from those who were to be part of the returning party (Ezra 2:59-62).

When Ezra the priest returned (Ezra 8:1 *ff.*) and learned that many of the exiles who had returned to the land of Judah earlier had married local wives, he was appalled because this seemed to him a profound threat to the purity of the faith (Ezra 9:1-4). After a public confession and a prayer of intercession, he issued a passionate plea for all those who had married foreign wives to put them away (Ezra 10:1-11). While a few objected (Ezra 10:15), it appears that most of the people agreed to do so (v. 12). While it appears that they did so, the text is not entirely clear (v. 17, for example, says "and by the first day of the first month they had finished dealing with all the men who had married foreign women," NIV). Ezra's concern in urging the divorce of these foreign women, however, is very clear. It is similar to the concern of the Greeks and Romans who were skeptical of marriage across class lines. "He represented a school of thought that saw survival in retrenchment and building a dam against floodwaters from without."[18] It appears, therefore, that when Ezra studied the law (Ezra 7:10), he may have been keenly fearful of the same dangers which befell ancient Israel when intermarriage with the Canaanites resulted in the growth of Baalism, disloyalty to Jahweh, and the growth of moral compromise. His encouragement of divorce, for those returning exiles who had contracted mixed marriages, therefore may have reflected a combination of ancient fears and contemporary cultural pressures. He may have seen marriage within the Jewish faith as the only way to preserve the integrity of the Hebrew faith.

What we may have between Malachi and Ezra is a kind of dialogue in which Malachi acknowledged the validity of the ancient concern expressed in the law and even the concern expressed at the time of Ezra but argued that the law against mixed marriages need not be interpreted in the same way at the time he wrote. Indeed, the prime concern of Malachi may have been to stem the tide of a rising divorce rate following the time and demands of Ezra.

Nehemiah seems closer to the position of Malachi than does Ezra, for while he did not approve of the mixed marriages of the returning exiles, he did not require those who had married foreign wives to divorce them. As Sigal says, Nehemiah's prime concern was not for a racially pure people, but for a holy community.[19] Nehemiah did report the promise of the returning exiles not to continue the practice of intermarriage with foreigners (Neh. 10:29). But while he recognized the continuation of the practice and condemned it strongly (Neh. 13:25*a* says, "I rebuked them and called curses down on them. I beat some of the men and pulled out their hair," NIV), he neither required nor asked them to divorce their wives. Beyond beating up a few of the men, all he did was to remind them of the sin that resulted from intermarriage with foreign women in the days of Solomon (Neh. 13:26). Therefore, when Malachi said that God hates divorce, he may have meant that God hates the fact that it was increasingly common.

The rarity of direct references to the practice of divorce in the Old Testament is paralleled by the paucity of comment on the problem or the practice in Jewish literature outside the Old Testament. What there is, however, suggests that divorce was uncommon in Judaism but that there was variety in the Hebrew understanding of the divorce law and in the application of that law. For example, on the one hand the Damascus Document, according to the interpretation of Philip Sigal, prohibited divorce and allowed remarriage only after the death of one's spouse.[20] The Damascus Document refers to some manuscripts discovered in a synagogue in Cairo, Egypt in 1896.[21] Fragments of the same materials were found among the Dead Sea Scrolls in the 1940s. This document appears to describe the rules governing a Jewish sect in the area of Damascus during the Babylonian captivity. According to O. Betz, the sect still flourished at the time of Jesus and belonged to the Essenes, a Jewish sect mentioned in the writings of the Jewish historian Josephus.[22] On the other hand, in the Elephantine community in Egypt, which has been described earlier, it appears that not only was remarriage allowed but also that the woman was free to initiate a divorce on an equal basis with the man.[23] Among the variety of Dead Sea Scrolls is a most unusual document dated about AD 134, a bill of divorce given to a husband by his wife. This bill suggests that at least in some circles of Judaism, the old custom of male exclusivism in the right of divorce was breaking down.[24]

In later Jewish tradition, divorce came to be regarded as an obligation under certain conditions. First, a man was obligated to divorce a bad wife. Though a bad wife is not described explicitly, some rabbis said that a man who lived with a bad wife would not go to hell because he had enough of that in life. Second, divorce came to be compulsory in the case of adultery. Third, divorce came to be compulsory in the case of sterility. However, neither desertion nor insanity were regarded as grounds for divorce in Jewish rabbinical tradition. In both these cases, the preservation of humane concern in Judaism is obvious.[25] As we shall argue, Jesus radically enlarged the humane element in Jewish tradition but altered other elements.

Remarriage

The law of Deuteronomy 24:1-4 makes it clear that, as a general rule, remarriage after divorce was permissible for either the husband or the wife. The only exception was that a woman whose second husband died or divorced her could not remarry her first husband. The reason for this exception or prohibition is not clear, but it may well have been intended to protect the woman from further humiliation by a former husband who had rejected her in the first place. Two examples in the Old Testament may seem to provide illustrations of other exceptions to the rule, but C. R. Taber is probably right in his contention that they really are not.[26] The first example is of Saul's giving of David's wife to another man (1 Sam. 25:44). Since David had not divorced Michal, he was legally justified in taking her back. The second example is Hosea, who apparently did divorce his wife. However, since we have no indication that she married another man, her return to Hosea was not a violation of the law either. It seems clear that, in both ancient Hebrew and Jewish tradition, remarriage after divorce was generally accepted and that the only exceptions to the rule were intended to protect the woman from humiliation and abuse.

Summary

Despite the strong emphasis on divorce as the privilege of the male, the dignity and freedom of the woman is also clearly recognized in the Old Testament. There is also strong emphasis on the unity of the family and the fidelity of both the husband and wife. It seems clear that the general assumption among the writers of the Old Testament was that divorce and remarriage, while allowed, should be the exception rather than the rule.

This notion is clearly supported by the fact that, despite the rabbinic debate between the schools of Hillel and Shammai, by the first century AD divorce was usually instituted on grounds of infidelity or adultery only.[27]

Notes

1. *The Interpreter's Dictionary of the Bible*, Supplementary Volume (Nashville: Abingdon Press, 1976), pp. 244-245.

2. Leonard Swidler, *Biblical Affirmations of Women* (Philadelphia: The Westminster Press, 1980), pp. 14-20.

3. O. J. Baab, *The Interpreter's Dictionary*, Vol. IV p. 297.

4. Phyllis Tribble, *God and the Rhetoric of Sexuality* (Philadelphia: Fortress Press, 1978), p. 73-102.

5. Ibid., p. 134.

6. Ibid., ch. 5.

7. Ibid., p. 196.

8. Swidler, pp. 1-10.

9. Baab, p. 865.

10. Tribble, p. 22.

11. Baab, p. 865.

12. See "The Numinous, the Sacred and the Holy in Scripture, *Biblical Theology*, Bulletin, October, 1982, p. 99.

13. Quoted from James B. Pritchard, *The Ancient Near Eastern Texts* (Princeton: University Press, 1958), pp. 170-171.

14. C. R. Taber, "Divorce," *The Interpreter's Dictionary*, Supplementary Volume, p. 245.

15. Johannes Pederson, *Israel: Its Life and Culture* (London: Oxford University Press, 1954), Vol. I, p. 71.

16. Philip Sigal, *The Emergence of Contemporary Judaism*, Volume One, *The Foundations of Judaism*, Part One (Pittsburg: The Pickwick Press, 1980), p. 114.

17. Ibid.

18. Ibid., p. 115.

19. Ibid., p. 120. Cf. Nehemiah 13:2-7.

20. Ibid.

21. See Leonhard Rost, *Judaism Outside the Hebrew Canon: An Introduction to the Documents* (Nashville: Abingdon Press, 1976), p. 170.

22. *The Interpreter's Dictionary*, Vol. I, p. 758.

23. See comment by Sigal, *The Emergence*, pp. 304, 350.

24. Ibid., p. 81.

25. Ibid., p. 332.

26. *The Interpreter's Dictionary*, Supplementary Volume, p. 245.

27. William Barclay, *The Gospel of Matthew*, revised edition, Vol. II (Philadelphia: Westminster, 1975), pp. 99, 206.

2
Divorce in the New Testament

In view of the fact that both divorce and remarriage are clearly allowed in the Old Testament, it is rather startling to find that many people believe the New Testament condemns both divorce and remarriage. Moreover, since in the context of Judaism the same understanding prevailed that we find in the Old Testament, Jesus' apparent views on divorce are more shocking to Jewish scholars today than most of his other teachings.

Whether the teaching on divorce represents a radical departure from the Jewish teaching remains to be seen. It is my contention that in some ways Jesus' teaching does go beyond Jewish teaching but that in other ways his viewpoint was surprisingly similar.

Clearly, traditional views of biblical teaching concerning divorce are being reviewed and reexamined by many biblical scholars. Robert F. Sinks and others are raising the general question, Might the primary concern of Jesus have been to attack the abuse of the divorce law rather than to attack the divorce law itself?[1]

Divorce in the Gospel of Mark

The Gospel of Mark appears to provide the earliest record of Jesus' teaching on divorce, and many scholars regard Mark's record as the fundamental source of our knowledge of Jesus' teaching on the subject because it is generally agreed to have been written first. Most scholars agree that Matthew and Luke followed Mark closely. Matthew 19 has convinced many scholars that Matthew's record differs from Mark's because Matthew was writing mainly for the Jewish community.

Before we attempt a judgment about that conclusion, let us take a look at Mark 10:2-12. To understand Mark's view one needs to note several points. First, Mark presents Jesus' teaching on divorce in the context of one of

29

several test questions the Pharisees asked Jesus. New Testament scholars generally agree that, at the time of Jesus, the dominant view was still that only a man could divorce his wife. Most commentators on this passage assume that the Pharisees were simply introducing the schools of conservative Shammai and liberal Hillel. The lack of specificity in the question as reported by Mark, however, may point to a different reason for asking the question. The way Mark reports the question by the Pharisees may be due to the fact that some were questioning the propriety of divorce for any reason. In that case, they may have anticipated that Jesus would present the very point of view he did present. His position appears to have placed him in a minority position and against the two mainstreams.

Second, however, it is significant to observe that Mark's report of Jesus' explanation of God's original reason for the law of divorce is the same as that assumed in Deuteronomy 24:1-3. That was to protect the dignity of woman from the hardheartedness of man (v. 5). However, Mark reports Jesus as going back beyond Deuteronomy in his interpretation of the original purpose of God in creation. While affirming the giving of the divorce law by God, Jesus said that God never intended for a *man* to divorce his wife. It seems possible that Jesus' prime interest was not to deal with the divorce law itself, but with the attitude of man to woman which made the divorce law necessary in the first place. Jesus may have been simply trying to correct a common view that woman was an object to be disposed of at man's pleasure. God joins man and woman together in marriage. Man should never reduce woman created in God's image to a position as an object.

However, verse 10 makes it clear that Jesus' response either disturbed or did not satisfy his disciples. When the Pharisees left, the disciples asked Jesus for further comment on the matter. His reply, reported in verses 11 and 12, has caused more anxiety among the divorced today than perhaps any other of Jesus' teachings. It has been the source of confusion and uncertainty not only among those who have been divorced and remarried but also among many pastors who try to minister to them. The embarrassing truth is that many divorcees who remarry fear, and are made to feel, that they are living in adultery.

Several questions may be raised about the meaning of the statement

"Whosoever shall put away his wife, and marry another, committeth adultery against her" (v.11). The first is whether Jesus was saying that man commits adultery against his wife by *putting away* his wife or by *marrying* another. It may make a considerable difference. If it were by putting her away that he commits adultery against her, then whether he marries another is irrelevant, for the sin is putting his wife away. In that case also to say that one who remarries is therefore living in adultery is a conclusion neither required nor justified by the text.

The second question is whether by marrying another the man committed adultery against his wife. In this case it would appear to mean that one who remarries is living in adultery, unless there may be some other way of translating *moichatai*. Since the word comes from an Old Testament word which is used in connection with idolatry and faithlessness, as well as sexual infidelity, it is difficult to say which came first. However, it would seem possible to translate the word as "breaks his commitment" to her. In that case, it is again possible to argue that the idea that one who remarries is henceforth living in adultery is a conclusion not required by the text. Despite the fact that no one to my knowledge translates *moichatai* any way but "commits adultery," the plain meaning appears to be that the husband has broken his original commitment, and the argument still is that to say he henceforth lives in adultery is a conclusion not required by the text. To break a covenant is condemned in the Old Testament and in the New Testament, but in neither case is it regarded as an unpardonable sin. I contend that to insist on an interpretation that views a divorced person who remarries as living in adultery makes remarriage an unpardonable sin. This interpretation seems to me to be in line with the argument of Edward Schweizer, in his comments on Matthew's version of Jesus' teaching on divorce in the Sermon on the Mount. Schweizer argues that Jesus' prime concern was with the one-sidedness of the decree which assumes that unless the man dissolves the marriage it is not dissolved. Thus, when a woman is rejected, she is driven to adultery.[2] Schweizer argues further that Jesus was not legalistic. He was only concerned to reject the male assumptions about their rights.[3] Similarly, William Barclay writes that in his rejection of divorce Jesus was laying down a principle, not a law. Further, he argues that Jesus did not even consider the divorce statement of

Moses a law, but a concession, due to the lost ideal expressed in Genesis.[4]

If we depend upon Mark, the only reasonable conclusion is that, in Jesus' view, God did not intend for a man to get rid of his wife for any reason or for a woman to divorce her husband. Many scholars believe the latter was added by Mark because he was writing for Romans who allowed women to initiate divorce proceedings.

This leaves some important questions unanswered however. What was the reason for the radical change from the Old Testament? This question may well be related to how we deal with other radical demands of Jesus, such as the rejection of violence (Matt. 5:38-39) and selling property (Luke 12:33).

Dwight Small solves the problem of Jesus' radical demands on divorce in a manner assumed by many on the other radical demands. He argues that the biblical tradition assumes that there are three ages in the moral development of man. First, there is the old age of the law. Second, there is the age of grace which came with the coming of Jesus and in which we are now living. Third, there is the age of the future kingdom. Small thinks that the divorce command of Jesus is intended for the age of the future kingdom. Therefore, we are correct in regarding the permanence of marriage with no divorce as the ideal. We are also justified in recognizing that we cannot universalize all the ethical teachings of Jesus in our time. This is an attractive approach, despite the fact that most New Testament scholars today would probably not support it.[5] There are other possibilities worth considering, however, as we shall see.

Divorce and Remarriage in Matthew's Gospel

Matthew mentioned the subject of divorce in two places. The first is in the Sermon on the Mount (Matt. 5—7), where he repeated the account of Mark on the subject with one simple addition. He inserted "saving for the cause of fornication" (5:32), which seems to soften Jesus' view and to allow for divorce and remarriage in case of sexual infidelity. Matthew 19 seems to be one of the most important passages in the New Testament on divorce and remarriage. Here Matthew repeated most of Mark 10:1-12. Several additions in Matthew's account, however, need examination.

Both Matthew and Mark presented Jesus' teaching on divorce as his response to the test question by the Pharisees. The first difference lies in the way the question was put. Mark reported that the Pharisees asked if it were permissible for a man to divorce his wife. Matthew added "for any cause" (19:3, RSV). It is not clear whether the way Matthew put it was intended to convey the notion that the Pharisees were asking if there were no grounds which make divorce justifiable or if any reasons the man chose were to be considered sufficient grounds. It seems likely that the intent was the latter since divorce was taken for granted as permissible. Despite this slight difference in the reported wording of the Pharisees' question thus far, Matthew represented no essential difference from Mark's account.

The second difference between Matthew's and Mark's accounts is that Matthew did not record Jesus' question about what Moses had commanded. This difference seems natural if, as generally is assumed, Matthew was writing mainly for Jewish readers because Jewish readers knew what the law prescribed and took the right of divorce for granted. What follows next in Matthew is essentially the same as in Mark, despite slight changes in the order. In both accounts, Jesus is reported as going behind the divorce law to the purpose of God in creation and saying that, since God joins husband and wife together, man should not separate them. Matthew and Mark were together also in reporting both the question as to why Moses gave the divorce law and the answer because of hardness of heart. Thus, it seems perfectly clear that, in reply to the questions asked of him about the legitimate grounds for divorce, Jesus began with a strong rejection of divorce on any grounds.

The third difference is the saving clause in Matthew 19:9: "Whoever divorces his wife except for unchastity, and marries another, commits adultery" (RSV). According to this phrase, in case of unchastity, both divorce and remarriage are permitted. Most New Testament scholars are agreed, however, that Matthew probably added this clause to make Jesus' teaching more acceptable to his Jewish readers. Fitzmeyer argues that the word *porneia,* translated *fornication* in the context of Matthew 19:9, refers to illicit kinship marriage. Thus, in his view, Matthew made an exception to Jesus' teaching on no divorce for Gentile Christians living in a Jewish Christian community. However, he also asks that if Matthew could make exceptions to deal with problems in his day, and Paul in his day, why cannot the church make exceptions for special problems confronting us today?[6] Although I have some uncertainty about the validity of Fitzmeyer's view about the interpretation of *porneia* in this context, his conclusion about making exceptions may have some merit. This argument appears to be based on an assumption which, though not stated by Fitzmeyer, is stated by both Barclay and Schweizer as mentioned earlier. The assumption is that Jesus was trying to stress the seriousness of the marriage commitment, while at the same time avoiding the legalism of the Pharisees.

The fourth difference follows in Matthew 19:10-15. This section has no parallel anywhere in the New Testament or in ancient Jewish literature. The famous eunuch saying here has often been interpreted in relation to the old Catholic ideal which came to exalt celibacy over marriage, but since verse 10 clearly connects this passage to the discussion of divorce, such a shift to an entirely different question seems unlikely. I maintain that here Matthew reported a saying of Jesus, perhaps not realizing at the time he wrote how significant the saying was in relation to his subject. It is quite probable that the conservative position that a man should divorce his wife only in case of infidelity was growing in popularity among the Jewish teachers. When Jesus rejected it, even his disciples were indignant. No wonder they said "If such is the case of a man with his wife, it is not expedient to marry" (v. 10, RSV). What they may have been saying was that if one cannot divorce his wife even for adultery, it would be better not to get married. Such a reply is understandable. Then Jesus' response is also understandable and should be interpreted in relation to the idea of infidelity not being grounds for a man divorcing his wife. Jesus' reply in verses 11-12 is very important, but I maintain is usually misinterpreted. "But he said to them, 'Not all men can receive this saying, but only those to whom it is given'" (v. 11, RSV). It seems possible to me that here Jesus was making a concession, not merely for Jews, but for *all* who find it difficult to accept or live up to the standard he set. Not everyone is given the power by emotional makeup, the circumstances of their marriage, or by the combination of frustrations they face to keep a marriage together.

"For there are eunuchs who have been so from birth, and there are eunuchs who have been made eunuchs by men, and there are eunuchs who have made themselves eunuchs for the sake of the kingdom of heaven"

(v. 12*a*, RSV). Barclay finds this eunuch statement puzzling and fails to relate it to the context. He argues that the verse 11 means that only Christians can live up to this standard Jesus set.[7] However, this seems to narrow the scope of Jesus' statement too much. Fortunately, Barclay also recognizes that Jesus laid down a principle, an ideal, and Barclay reminds us that we err in making it a law.

Edward Schweizer linked the eunuch saying with the divorce material, yet he fails to note clearly the possible connection between the radical rule and the concession Jesus made in saying, "He who is able to receive this, let him receive it" (v. 12*b*, RSV).[8]

It seems to me that in this eunuch passage Jesus may well be following his recognition that some cannot live up to his ideal by giving sample examples which were intended as suggestive, but surely not all-inclusive. Some men are sexually impotent and not physically qualified for consummating marriage. Other men in ancient times were castrated to become servants in the king's harem. Ahab, for example, had many wives and eunuchs. Still others lived as eunuchs (celibate—unmarried) because of choices they made in their own vocation. Jeremiah was an example. Some notable men throughout Christian history have lived celibate lives, not because they thought that made them superior, but for various other reasons. Kierkegaard never married because, with his emotional problems, he figured he would not make a good husband. He was probably right. Jesus may have been saying that some people should not get married. Others cannot keep a marriage together. Some can. Those who can, should. That may be what he meant by the final statement: "He who is able to receive this, let him receive it." Who knows who can keep a marriage together and who cannot? Perhaps only God and the persons involved, and sometimes the persons involved do not know. In view of this possibility, the rest of us would do well to be slow to pass judgment on the divorced.

Divorce According to Paul

While Paul never directly mentioned the sayings of Jesus on divorce that are reported in the Gospels, it seems likely that he was familiar with them. I contend that, in general terms, Paul's views were essentially the same as those of Jesus. In fact many New Testament scholars agree that 1

Corinthians 7:10-11 is the earliest recorded witness to Jesus' teaching on divorce. Paul's statement may, therefore, be grounded in the same source as Mark 10:2-19. It is also widely agreed that, like Mark, Paul was writing with the Gentile community in mind. Both he and Mark may have had in mind, however, a set of contextual problems which are more apparent in 1 Corinthians than in Mark.

The problems appear to be twofold. One problem was whether, in view of the uncertainty and shortness of time, one should make any changes in the status of one's life after becoming a Christian. It appears indeed that four types of persons were involved in this question. First Gentiles were considering whether, in the face of Jewish pressure, to become circumcised. (v. 18) Second, single persons were considering marriage. (v. 1) Third, slaves were considering whether to acquire freedom. Fourth, married women who had become Christians wondered whether the radical demands of the Christian calling required a break with the marriage relationship, especially if one's mate were not a Christian. Paul's general advice seems to have been that the call to follow the risen Lord requires none of these things, but that one should concentrate on being obedient.

However, from the way Paul interpreted and applied the meaning of obedience to several quite different situations in a variety of ways, he clearly seemed reluctant to make a hard-and-fast rule. Paul was not a legalist because he did not understand Jesus to be a legalist. The inflexible principle Paul invoked is faithfulness to God in whatever state one is in. What that requires is in some measure determined by the immediate situation. While the application of this principle of fidelity to God sounds and is somewhat flexible, Paul placed limits on its flexibility, as we shall see. One other point should be noted. Many New Testament scholars believe that a number of things Paul said in his early writings reflect his belief in the imminent return of Christ and the end of history. In that case, some of his own views would have to be defined differently in terms of their applicability for today's situation. It is in this context that we should interpret Paul's particular comments on marriage, separation, and singleness.[9]

Paul began chapter 7 by saying, in effect, that the single life is good but that just as marriage is not for everyone neither is the single life. In fact

Paul clearly supported marriage. To those who were trying to decide whether to get married, Paul gave his counsel, but he made a clear distinction between what he regarded as counsel and what is to be regarded as command (cf. v. 6,10). His counsel was that they should not get married. Clearly, however, he did not intend this counsel be taken as a rule. Verse 28 reads, "But if you should marry, you have not sinned" (NASB). His counsel to the married was that they should not break up the marriage because of religious differences if the unbeliever were willing to continue the marriage (v. 11-12). Paul stated the general principle which should govern one's decision to make changes in the manner of life in verse 24, "Brethren, let each man remain with God in that condition in which he was called" (NASB). The whole context of his discussion suggests that, in Paul's view, one should keep changes in life situations to a minimum because of the imminence of the end of history. This fact has significant bearing on verse 11, where Paul wrote, "but if she does leave, let her remain unmarried, or else be reconciled to her husband" (NASB). It may be that this is a command that was time bound, applicable only in Paul's day.

I recall Gaines S. Dobbins reminding us of the need to distinguish between those teachings of Paul that were time serving and those that are of continuing importance. Verse 26 gives some foundation for the argument that Paul himself recognized such a distinction. Paul was not really addressing himself to the problems of divorce and remarriage which we see in society today. We must preserve commitment to the principles he laid down, but not to the concrete instructions he gave for problems peculiar perhaps to the church at Corinth.

One of the central principles of Paul that is of continuing significance is the principle of freedom (v.32). In touching on several questions in this chapter, Paul's prime concern was to keep one's calling as a Christian central. The center of one's concern was to be this Christian calling. One should be free of those concerns which hinder giving one's best in his (or her) calling. Today, the use of this principle may well justify both divorce and remarriage in some instances. An example would be where irreconcilable differences result in the destruction of a marriage relationship and distraction from one's responsibility as a Christian. In that case, divorce might give expression to the principle because, in society today, there are at least sometimes when "two are better than one" (see Eccl. 4:9-10).

In verses 38 and 39, Paul may appear to contradict the argument presented here, but I do not really think so. He simply repeated his commitment as a Hebrew to the law of divorce stated both in Deuteronomy and in different form by the teaching of Jesus. In his view, woman should look on marriage as a lifelong commitment. There is no clear evidence anywhere in his writing, however, that Paul rejected the law of divorce and remarriage as stated in Deuteronomy as a matter of principle. What he did reject, as Jesus did, is the taking of the marriage commitment lightly. He said that one who makes a commitment in marriage should not break it, but he left room for assuming that, when the commitment is broken by either partner, it is broken. Paul never commented on the theoretical question of infidelity as a ground for divorce and remarriage. But it appears to me that if he had, he would have applied the principles of freedom and responsibility in such a way as to justify both divorce and remarriage in some instances.

In summary, while Paul clearly discouraged both divorce and remarriage, he no more condemned them as a matter of principle than he condemned marriage as a matter of principle. The fact that he never gave an explicit answer to the problem may mean that the questions of divorce and remarriage in principle were not the central questions in his mind.

Romans 7

When Paul wrote in verse 2 that a married woman is bound by her husband as long as he lives, his central interest was not divorce and remarriage, but was rather to give an illustration of the relation between the law and the believer in Christ (vv. 1-3).[10] His argument was that just as under the law a woman was bound to a man for life (unless *he* divorced *her*), so a man was bound to the law in a variety of ways. However, since the coming of Christ, Paul said, "But now we have been released from the Law, having died to that by which were bound, so that we serve in newness of the Spirit and not in oldness of the letter" (v. 6, NASB). To focus attention on verses 2-3 as grounds for arguing against divorce and remarriage would, therefore, distort Paul's whole purpose and meaning in this section. The contrast between the law which binds one to legal regulations and the Spirit which sets one free is the central point Paul was making; and to interpret verses 2-3 as literally applicable today would contradict the argument Paul was making. This is an important point if, as many New Testament scholars agree, Paul's letter to the Romans reflects his maturest thought and is the nearest thing we have in all his letters to a systematic summary of his views, based on long and careful reflection.

1 Timothy 3:2,12

Since this passage speaks of both bishops (pastors) and deacons (servants) as required to be the husbands of one wife, it is often interpreted as condemning the practice of ordaining men as pastors or as deacons who have been divorced. Aside from the value of having pastors and deacons serve as ideal role models, this argument is difficult to support since the question has been debated for centuries with no clear consensus resulting. Most scholars reject the notion that the writer had in mind the condemnation of remarriage after divorce. It is more likely that he was condemning celibacy as a requirement for the clergy.[11] He may also have been saying a pastor or a deacon should not be a polygamist. It is unclear whether he would have approved their membership in the church. While polygamy was not common in the Judaism of New Testament times or in the Gentile community of the Roman world, it did exist. Though never condemned explicitly in the New Testament, it has been generally, though not universally, condemned throughout Christian history. Clearly, polygamy was taken for granted and widely practiced in early Hebrew history. However, it seems to have become increasingly rare by the end of the Old Testament era, and the early church condemned it. It seems likely that the concern of the writer in 1 Timothy 3:2,12 was to discourage the spread of the practice of polygamy at least among the leadership of the church. In view of the disposition of the church toward polygamy throughout its history, the purpose of the author seems to have been very effective. Therefore, I conclude that this passage has no relevance to the question of divorce and remarriage.

The Problem of Interpretation

One final point needs to be made. The whole problem of the ideal of permanence in marriage which we have found in Jesus' teaching must be considered in the context of the broad question of how we interpret the ethical ideals of Jesus on other matters. An example is violence. New Testament scholars generally agree today that Jesus clearly discouraged violence among his followers and that the early church interpreted this to mean that a Christian could not participate in the military. However, it is equally clear that most of the churches changed their views on this issue and that, although the church generally still discourages violence, it does not usually discriminate against those who have participated in it, either officially as policemen or soldiers or unofficially in cases of self-defense or defense of a neighbor. My argument is that failure to live up to the ideal in a particular situation creates a need for forgiveness but is not a ground for condemnation or discrimination. Therefore, to treat divorcees as failures as persons is wrong. They are not more failures as persons than the rest of us, for we all have sinned and come short of the glory of God. Those whose marriages have failed should not be condemned by the rest of us. Surely Jesus would say of the divorcee as readily as the adulteress, "Neither do I condemn thee: go, and sin no more" (John 8:11). Remarriage for the divorcee, like remarriage for the widow or widower or for the never married, may or may not be a sin, depending on the circumstances, the motive, the maturity of the persons involved or the commitment they demonstrate.

How this argument relates to specific situations will be discussed in the chapter on grounds for remarriage by a divorcee. My conclusion is that many individual Christians and many churches need to change their attitude toward people who are divorced and to those who remarry after being divorced. Finally, I would encourage those who have condemned themselves and have accepted the condemnation of others because they have been divorced and remarried to stop condemning themselves and believe the good news of the gospel: on the basis of their repentance they are forgiven their sins just as are the rest of us who have never been divorced. They, with the rest of us, are to seek the leadership of the Spirit as we seek in obedience to Jesus Christ to find the will of God for our lives, step by step. Whether unmarried, married, divorced, or remarried, the call of Jesus Christ is to follow him as best we can in a world that makes that objective a very difficult one to achieve.

Notes

1. Sinks, Robert F., "A Theology of Divorce," *Christian Century,* April 20, 1977, p. 377.
2. Schweizer, Edward, *The Good News According to Matthew* (Atlanta: John Knox Press, 1975), p. 126.
3. Ibid., p. 383.
4. Barclay, William, *The Gospel of Matthew* (Philadelphia: Westminster Press, 1975), Vol. II, p. 200.
5. Small, Dwight, *The Right to Remarry* (Old Tappan, N.J.: Fleming H. Revell, 1975).
6. Fitzmeyer, Joseph A., "Matthean Divorce Texts and some New Palestinian Evidence," *Theological Studies,* June 1976, pp. 224-225.
7. Ibid., pp. 207-208.
8. Schweizer, p. 382.
9. Craig, C. T., *The Interpreter's Bible* (Nashville: Abingdon, 1953), Vol. X, p. 76.
10. Sandy, W., and Headlam, A. C., *Romans,* International Critical Commentary, (Edinburgh: T & T Clark, 1911), p. 171.
11. *The Interpreter's Bible* (New York: Abingdon, 1955) Vol. XI, p. 410.

3
Considering Getting a Divorce

People have different styles when it comes to making decisions. The decision of whether to divorce is a complex decision. Some people may consider getting a divorce a long time before doing anything about it or communicating the consideration with her or his spouse. For others the decision to divorce will be sudden and impulsive.

If you are considering divorce, there are some factors which are worth careful attention. In this chapter, the concern is to invite both the impulsive and reflective decision makers to consider a number of things before making a decision to divorce or to announce a divorce.

There are two reasons for this invitation. The first is that once the decision and/or the announcement is made, damage may be done to the relationship which cannot be undone. The second reason is that some studies show that many who divorce report that if they had it to do over, they would not go through with it. Some of the factors in such regrets may be useful for those who have not gone so far in the decision that they cannot turn back. Unfortunately, not much research has been done on the process of marriage breakups.[1] Much of what has been written is based on reports of the process after the fact. Moreover, much of what is reported by couples in the process of breaking up their marriages is difficult to evaluate objectively either by the couples or by their counselors. Nevertheless, from research that has been done, from my own experience as a counselor and as a participant observer, and from my outlook as a student of Christian ethics, it seems necessary to point to several questions an individual or a couple considering a divorce might do well to consider. Part of my concern here is to help those who might otherwise make an impulsive decision they might regret after it is too late to back out. It is to encourage them to give more thought to their decision and action by examining the road ahead, including the alternatives and consequences. To be sure, one cannot know all the answers to questions that might be raised at this stage. Thus, consideration of the problems and prospects may be no more than educated guesses. Nevertheless, I maintain that it is our Christian moral responsibility to imagine the possible consequences of any and all of our moral actions, despite the uncertainties involved.

Perhaps the foremost question in the decision-making process is whether the marriage can be saved. What is the condition of the marriage? In this chapter, I suggest some considerations which both marriage partners as individuals can look at. Assessing the condition of a marriage can be helped greatly by involving a third party. The merits of the marriage partners receiving counseling individually and as a couple are discussed in this chapter also. In considering divorce, economic questions are important. The chapter concludes with a consideration of the economic aspects of divorce.

What Are the Possibilities?

Perhaps the most important question one considering a divorce should ask is, What are the possibilities for saving the marriage, for enduring or resolving the difficulties? Consideration of the possibilities includes several closely related questions. The first of these questions is, Where are we in our marriage? It appears that in some cases people live together in an odd kind of dependency relationship who, nevertheless, remain strangers throughout their lives, as Eric Fromm says.[2] Others come to know each other with at least relative accuracy and discover they do not really like each other and decide, therefore, they will no longer love each other. Sometimes an individual will make such a decision. This situation puts the other partner in an impossible position. Still others, because of obstacles which develop in communication, reach a kind of a stalemate in the development of both self-knowledge and the knowledge of the other person.

For example one woman in a recent counseling session said to me, "I simply do not know where I stand with him. It would help to know, but I cannot get him to talk. He just clams up." Then she went on, "I just don't know how much more I can take." Part of my task was to help her find out whether she could take any more and whether she really wanted to endure what was necessary. A popular magazine has a regular section entitled "Can This Marriage Be Saved?" Without saying so in those exact words, the woman I just mentioned was asking that very question. It was my task to help her answer the question. In her case at this point the answer seems positive, for real progress seems to be in the making.

Others with whom I have counseled have reached a negative answer to the question because of what appeared to be irreconcilable differences. I have a friend who is a minister of counseling in a local church. He often has couples referred to him by a local judge who, in many cases, refuses to grant a divorce decree until the couple has sought counseling. According to my friend, however, the problem with that is that the counseling usually is unsuccessful in preventing the divorce because by the time the couple goes to court their minds are made up; they do not wish to be talked out of their decision. It may be that many who need counseling are more hesitant than they should be about seeking it from a minister because they fear that he or she will try to talk them out of it. I strongly suspect, however, that many couples get divorced before they really know their own minds, and then it is sometimes too late to back out.

What I am suggesting is that, if you are considering getting a divorce and are not sure of what you want to do, you do not hesitate to go to a minister for help. Even if you cannot take his or her counsel, you may be able to make your own decision better after talking to someone. Whether you seek counsel or not, it is important that you ask yourself where you are. Several persons with whom I have counseled after their divorces have said that, after reflection, they would recommend that all persons considering divorce get counseling both before and after the divorce.

When is a marriage broken? In general terms, I would answer that a marriage is broken when the relationship between husband and wife is damaged beyond repair. While it is not possible to define the criteria which indicate irreparable damage to the satisfaction of everyone, it appears to me that several criteria are basic. The first of these criteria is communication. When communication has broken down, the marriage may be in serious trouble. Even bad communication may be better than no communication at all. Some couples hastily conclude that the marriage is gone simply because they engage in verbal fights. Verbal fights may be futile when they do not resolve anything because they merely vent hostility without getting at the problem. They may be fruitful, however, when, by their means, a sensitive partner gets clues to his or her problems (or both) and is willing to do something creative to solve them.

Sometimes there is nothing quite like a good verbal fight to clear the air. The movie *The Graduate*—while a sad, horrible story in many respects— dramatically demonstrates both the tragedy and the possibility of verbal battles between a couple who had not learned the importance of honest and creative communication. There may still be hope for a marriage where a good deal of dialogue occurs, even though it is disagreeable. The fact is that many persons find the truth too painful to communicate except under pressure. Therefore, the experience of communication problems is not necessarily the death knell of a marriage as long as efforts at communication continue. If both partners are willing, who knows? Something good may come out of it. In this regard, Reuel Howe's book *The Miracle of Dialogue* may be a useful tool for couples who are willing to work at resolving their communication problem.

When communication breaks down completely, however, the marriage may be in serious trouble. Even here, however, it seems important to observe that temporary lapses may not be serious signs at all, but when a partner says to me, as several have, "I cannot ever get him (or her) to talk to me about anything anymore; he (or she) just clams up," the marriage may be in serious trouble. Unfortunately, it takes two to communicate; when one is willing and the other is unwilling or unable to communicate about the problems any longer, the marriage may be damaged beyond repair.

A second criterion for a badly damaged marriage is closely related to the problem of communication. It has to do with the interference with one's normal responsibilities as a person, either at home or at work. If the relationship is so strained that either or both partners is unable or unwilling to carry out the routine responsibilities of home life, the marriage may be in serious trouble. The responsibilities range from meeting each other's sexual needs to taking out the garbage. In Tennessee Williams's play *Cat on a Hot Tin Roof,* the wife of Big Daddy said, as she patted the bed, that when a marriage went on the rocks the rocks were right there. She was oversimplifying a complex problem, but the experience of many counselors supports the view that there is often an interrelationship between the responsibility of meeting each other's sexual needs and many other responsibilities around the home.

One wife told her counselor that long before the divorce she had been so badly hurt by her husband that when they made love, she felt nothing anymore. In fact, she said she could no longer stand for him even to touch her. Her marriage was in serious trouble. Failure in one area of responsibility may feed failure in other areas. When the strains in the marriage relationship interfere with the performance of one's responsibility in the office or work place, we have an equally serious indication. Sometimes an employer will suspect some personal or family difficulty in the life of an employee because of work performance. In some cases, family problems have become so acute that employees have lost their jobs because of the way family problems reduce the efficiency of performance. When one's work relationship is threatened by marital difficulty, something must be done.

A third criterion for determining the seriousness of the damage done to a marriage relationship is closely related to the problem of effect on responsibility and may, indeed, be the root difficulty in causing damage to the performance of one's responsibilities. I refer to the personal stress level. An individual considering a divorce because of marriage difficulties may ask, How much more of this can I take? Symptoms of excessive stress may include high blood pressure, nervousness, indigestion, insomnia, physical exhaustion, tendency to eat or drink too much. When the stress level in either or both partners in the marriage is so high that the emotional, psychological, and physical condition of both partners suffers, something must be done. Either the relationship must be improved or broken.

Closely related in many instances where there are children is the question of the effects of continuation of a bad marriage on the emotional lives of the children. This is a very difficult matter to assess, as we shall see later, but it must be pointed out here that the time may come when the couple must weigh the comparative damage of a bad marriage on the children with the damage that a separation and divorce might have on the children. Some recent studies seem to indicate that not only do some children blame themselves for their parents' divorce but also some children never get over their parents' divorce. The damage of the divorce on their emotional lives may be with them as long as they live. Others argue that some children of divorce often adjust quite well, and, in fact, can live normal, productive, and happy lives.

The choice between continuing a bad marriage for the sake of the children and breaking it up for the sake of the children is not an easy one, and there is no simple rule that I can suggest to resolve the dilemma for anyone. However, while this criterion is not the only one in considering the possibility of a divorce, the question of what is best for the children seems to me to be one of the questions one should ask. The fact is that once a marriage has degenerated in the ways already described, emotional damage has been done to the children involved, so the basic question still to be faced is how the couple or the individual can prevent the damage from increasing in the future. A closely related question is, Which route, keeping the marriage together or separating, would promise the greatest possibility for repairing the damage that has been done? I would not want to press my argument here too strongly, however, for there comes a time when the parents can no longer bear the responsibility for repairing the damage done to the children. Sometimes the children take the divorce in better stride than parents indicate. When divorce has been decided on, however, parents should help the children prepare for it, though many children see it coming even before their parents do.

Some of my friends who waited until the children were out on their own to get a divorce expected shock and disappointment when they announced their decision to their children. To their amazement their children were disappointed, but not surprised. Moreover, they accepted their parents' divorce readily and continued to love them both. Each of their children is happily married and seem to have learned from their parents' mistakes.

A final criterion for determining the status of the marriage is the effect of the problems experienced in marriage on the religious life. This was, as indicated in chapter 2, a prime concern of Paul as he considered the questions of whether in his time and from his perspective single persons should get married and whether married persons who become Christians should continue to live with an unbelieving partner. Paul's answer was that, if the unbeliever were willing to continue to live with the believer, the believer should continue the marriage. Paul's general answer to the question of getting married or staying married was the same as his answer to the question of changing one's social status in other ways: one should make no unnecessary changes. The reason for Paul's position may have been his belief in the nearness of the end of all things. Still, I cannot avoid the conclusion that sensing the uncertainty of human knowledge of the times, Paul added what I consider to be the abiding principle which was his central concern. That is that the prime concern of one's life should be the Christian calling which affects the whole of life. Whatever one does affects that calling and should be affected by it.

While Paul's interest in the question of whether to get married or stay married, according to how the answer affected one's vocation, may not seem relevant to our time, it really is quite relevant. Today, being married or staying married can either enhance one's Christian vocation, as many ministers have found, or can be a painful distraction, as many others have found. Paul made it very clear that one who is married has responsibilities in addition to one's Christian vocation that a single person does not. He was probably discussing this problem from his own perspective as one who was single at the time. (It is not necessary to our purpose here to speculate on whether or not Paul had been married.) A single person as an itinerant missionary could travel easier than one who had a wife and children. It is still so. Sometimes the advantages and disadvantages of each (married or single) may outweigh the other, depending on the circumstances. It seems to me that the point Paul was making is very clear and simple: what one is considering should be decided in part by how it may affect the continuation and effective expression of the commitment to Jesus Christ that has been made. While Paul never commended getting out of a marriage because of religious differences and while he did commend the acceptance of marriage responsibilities, he clearly placed commitment to Christ at the top of the list of priorities.

Paul, of course, was writing in 1 Corinthians about a narrow set of questions. He never really touched on the variety of marital problems faced by many today. I am convinced, nevertheless, that the same principle Paul established for considering the two decisions about marriage I have mentioned, is applicable to the problem of many who are considering getting divorced today. One question to be put to many today should be, What effect would the continuation of this marriage have on your spiritual life and, in case there are children, on the spiritual lives of the children? There may be cases where the dominance of one partner who is not Christian is so overpowering as to make any spiritual influence in the family setting virtually impossible. Thus, another question might be, Would breaking up the marriage make possible the preservation of the spiritual life?

A very common complaint of married persons considering divorce concerns the immaturity of their mates. Frequently this immaturity is, at least in part, spiritual immaturity. Many couples come to difficulty in their marriages because one partner continues to grow spiritually, intellectually, and emotionally while the other stays the same or grows stale. Suddenly sometimes, parents discover that they have been so busy providing economic support and intellectual and spiritual materials for the growth of their children that they have neglected their own growth. Often the discovery will be that one partner has grown with the children, and the other has not. A friend whose children are grown, who is still living with her husband, and who has no thought of divorce reported this problem. One day she realized that she was sitting at breakfast with a stranger. Because of their mutual Christian commitment, she and her husband have stayed together. In other instances I have known, similar variations in growth resulted in divorce.

I am not aware of studies which examine the effect of spiritual disparity between husbands and wives on both the couple and the children's spiritual life, but I rather suspect that in many cases, even where couples stay together, the damage is considerable. What some have to ask is whether keeping the marriage together would make Christian commitment and growth impossible or whether breaking up the marriage would assure continued spiritual commitment and growth. There is perhaps no simple and easy answer. Each individual must decide how the principle I have stated applies to his or her unique situation.

An additional fundamental question, which should be considered in deciding this issue of how to apply the principle I have stated, is, How do you handle the guilt one feels because of difficulties developing in the marriage? Guilt is a very serious reality. When considering divorce, the marriage partner should ask whether everything possible has been done to effect one's own spiritual growth and the growth of the partner. It is to be recognized, of course, that one who is embroiled in the emotional upheaval of marital stress may not be able to evaluate personal guilt accurately. A counselor may be needed. Some marriage partners I have known condemned themselves unduly. Others have been inclined to evade responsibility.

A very important question which marriage partners need to ask themselves is, could my own spiritual and emotional immaturity be the main problem in my marriage? Most of us find it easy to see the faults of others while we are blind to our own. What is worse, we sometimes are most sensitive to those particular failures of others which are in fact the very "sins which so easily beset us." Many people who want to break up their marriages are so inclined because they have problems that are both spiritual and neurotic; for them, getting out of the marriage is a neurotic solution. This point is well made in the book *Divorce Won't Help* by Edmund Bergler (N.Y.: Harper and Brothers, 1948).

From the Christian perspective, the central question underlying all these factors is whether—in the face of frustrations, crises, and differences that have developed in the marriage—the couple can live up to the ideal for marriage set forth by Jesus. As stated in chapter 2, some can, and some cannot. Perhaps in some cases, only the couple and God know whether the marriage can be saved and the Christian ideal realized. Perhaps in some instances only God knows. Certainly some individuals I have known were not sure whether their marriage could be saved. As a counselor, I have had uncertainty in my mind as to whether particular marriages could or should be continued. My understanding of the teachings of Jesus and Paul, however, suggests that each individual should try to keep his or her marriage together.

There may be cases, however, where it is neither desirable nor possible to continue the marriages. A basic reason is that the continuation of a bad marriage or the restoration of a successful marriage in either case requires the cooperation and creative efforts of both partners. One alone cannot keep a marriage together. Another reason it is difficult or impossible to keep a marriage together is the persistence of irreconcilable differences. When two people, who have serious incompatibilities, are unwilling or unable to change and continue to live together to honor one Christian ideal, they may find themselves violating other Christian ideals despite their honest efforts to avoid doing so. Quite frankly, some have made convincing arguments to me that they had to get out of bad marriages to salvage what Christian commitment they had. I am convinced, moreover, that some, as Jesus and Kierkegaard implied, should not get married. For those who should not get married and do so anyway, bringing the marriage to an end may be the merciful thing to be done for both persons.

Considering Counseling

An amazing variety of persons are now giving advice and counsel to people who are experiencing marital difficulty. In the concluding section of this chapter, I wish to make some simple suggestions to the marriage partners and to those who give them counsel. To the marriage partners I would suggest that you go to a good counselor before your marriage gets to the stage where you seriously consider divorce. The reason to seek counseling early is that, by the time you seriously consider divorce the rift in your marriage may be too great. The question of when to go to a counselor is difficult to answer. A simple suggestion would be that the time to go to a counselor is when you have done all you can think of to patch up your bad marriage and nothing works or when the stress level is too high, as suggested earlier.

The question of what kind of counselor to seek is even more difficult to answer. My first inclination would be to suggest seeking a Christian counselor because such a one who has good training and insight would be ideal. Some Christian counselors, however, are as legalistic as the Pharisees who were partly responsible for the crucifixion of Jesus. They contradict the spirit and the teachings of Jesus by the legalistic approach they use. They are neither good counselors nor good interpreters of the New Testament. There are plenty of Christian counselors, however, who are both well trained in their understanding of personality, the techniques of counseling, and in their understanding of biblical teachings.

Some secular counselors not only have no real respect for the Christian tradition but also they regard any commitment to the Christian faith as a form of sickness. A counselor with such a viewpoint could provide little or no help for the person who has serious problems with their understanding of the teachings of the Bible. Other secular counselors, however, have a healthy respect for the role the Christian faith plays in the life of a believer, and would not suggest that one violate his or her own beliefs. Some secular counselors (including clinical psychologists and psychiatrists) moreover can help one sort out and recognize the variety of conflicting emotions that may hinder one's self-understanding and a constructive response to one's marital difficulties. Although the Christian faith must be related to the totality of one's life, there are some problems which are not specifically Christian problems and help from a non-Christian may be just as effective as from a Christian counselor. Examples are the defense mechanisms we often use without realizing it. Any good clinical psychologist or psychiatrist, regardless of their religious orientation, could help us to recognize and deal with them.

To those who consider counseling with persons who are experiencing marital difficulty and are in the early stages of thinking about divorce, I would make several modest suggestions. The first is obvious but may bear repeating because it can easily be forgotten. A counselor cannot save a marriage. He can, with care and encouragement, help the couple or an individual partner come to a more adequate view of where they are. But to assume that he must save the marriage is to take on a superhuman responsibility. If the marriage fails, he has set himself up for a heavy burden of false guilt. Second, and closely related, do not try to make the decision about staying in or getting out of the marriage for the person or persons involved. This is difficult sometimes because the counselor may be asked directly: "What do you think I should do?" The counselor should not usually answer this question directly at all. A basic reason is that if he or she does and the counselee takes the advice given and later has reason to regret it, the counselor may be blamed. Third, and again closely related, the counselor would do well to keep the responsibility for decision making squarely on the shoulders of the person being counseled. The role of the counselor in trying to help a person considering divorce should be concentrated on helping the person clarify the biblical teachings, his own mind and emotions, the alternative possibilities, and consequences. Finally, the counselor should encourage the person considering divorce to seek a redemptive solution. This suggestion may appear to contradict the first one about not feeling obligated to save the marriage, but the difference is that this suggestion focuses on the responsibility of the counselee rather than on the counselor. The person seeking counsel should be encouraged to do whatever he or she thinks is the most redemptive thing to do for the marriage, for the other partner, and for the individual. The counselor should not feel obligated to give solutions but should be a caring friend helping another person to clarify his or her own problems, needs, and possibilities. The counselor's own ethical ideals may be stated but should not be imposed on the other persons in the counseling relationship.

Economic Costs

Although the liberalization of laws relating to divorce in many states has made the cost of a divorce much cheaper than it was a few years ago, the economic costs in many instances turn out to be greater than either of the persons involved anticipated. For example, many discover to their amazement the economic truth of the author of Ecclesiastes: "Two are better than one." They discover that the equitable division of assets that often follows the breakup of a marriage is very difficult to achieve to the mutual, individual satisfaction. Further, the legal costs, though in many instances less in comparison with other costs, are considerable in some cases. Who deserves most of the property? Can either partner survive on an income and/or a piece of property that has been divided? The fact is that some couples do not count the cost of a divorce, not only in terms of money but also in terms of the increased stress that economic anxiety will bring. You may believe that the freedom from the emotional strain of the marriage may be worth the economic sacrifice involved, and it well may be. In some cases I have no doubt that it is. In some cases I have known, however, I have suspected that the economic anxiety which followed the separation and divorce was far greater than was anticipated.[3] One who is considering breaking up a marriage should give serious thought to the economic problem to be faced.

Several specific questions need to be considered. First, What is the specific cost of getting a divorce in terms of lawyer's fees? Bustanoby gives an excellent summary of legal cost estimates in various states. The range is from $200 to $2,000.[4] While it is true that legal services in noncriminal cases are available on a sliding scale for those who cannot afford private attorneys, many who are really in need will find it difficult to secure this aid for two reasons. First, the regional offices of Legal Services are scattered and sometimes out of reach of those who need them. Second, federal and local funding cuts in recent years together with the very large volume of cases the average Legal Services office handles result in a priority listing of the types of cases a local office chooses to handle. Divorce cases may not even be on the list. Even those offices which handle divorce cases often have a very large backlog and may take months or years getting to your case.

In case you are considering employing an attorney, check with a minister or other friend who is knowledgeable about the fees, efficiency, and professional competency of local attorneys. Many attorneys charge an hourly rate, but some are far more efficient than others. Make sure you have a clear understanding of the costs *before* you get head over heels in debt. If there are any disagreements between the husband and the wife over the terms of the separation and divorce, there is wisdom in each partner having a separate attorney. Despite the first appearance of double and unnecessary expense, having separate attorneys might turn out to be the most economical route, especially for the one who otherwise might have come out on the short end of the legal settlement. Though you may think you cannot afford an attorney, it may turn out that you cannot afford to be without one. In most communities, moreover, there are a few lawyers who will handle hardship cases without charge. For most people who get a divorce, nevertheless, there are attorneys' fees to be paid. If you are considering a divorce, then again I urge that you consider whether you can afford it. More detailed suggestions about consulting an attorney will be given in the next chapter.

A second economic question one should ask is, Can I afford separate maintenance. One has to move out, and many couples have grown so accustomed to the economic advantages of life together that they are not prepared for the economic shock of separate maintenance. With the increasing number of working wives in today's marketplace, divorces are sometimes sought hastily because individuals think they can afford separate maintenance. Others, though they know they can probably afford it but recognizing the economic inconveniences separation would involve, work harder at keeping the marriage together. Often the wives return to the home of parents, frequently at a time when parents can ill afford to resume economic responsibility. One who is considering this route should consider the ethics of such a decision. In my opinion, those who leave home and then return are justified in doing so only in circumstances of temporary emergency or in cases where there will be mutual economic benefit to the parents and the child whose marriage is broken. In either case, the return should be with the full agreement of the parents.

The question of separate economic maintenance, furthermore, includes the long-range question of plans for self-support. Many wives and mothers who count on alimony and child support after the divorce are often greatly disappointed. Those who do have good prospects of alimony for a stated period, and child support where there are children, should plan immediately to get any necessary training to prepare for the end of both alimony and child-support payments. In every community of any size, there are people who have made the transition from married to single status. There are advantages in seeking their counsel, but they often may be less objective than a professional counselor. You might do well, therefore, to have the information and counsel they give you evaluated by your minister or another counselor who has professional training.

Notes

1. George Levinger and Oliver C. Moles, editors, *Divorce and Separation: Conditions, Causes and Consequences* (New York: Basic Books, 1979), p. 38 *ff.*
2. Eric Fromm, *The Art of Loving* (New York: Bantam Books, 1967), p. 74.
3. R. Lofton Hudson, *Til Divorce Do Us Part* (New York: Thomas Nelson Sons, 1973).
4. Andre Bustanoby, *But I Didn't Want a Divorce* (Grand Rapids: Zondervan, 1978), chapter 3.

4
Problems in the Process of Divorce: Legal, Moral, Spiritual

One of the problems some divorcees discover after it is too late is that they have made decisions that complicate their lives as much or more than the bad marriages they were trying to escape. As indicated earlier, some studies have shown that, for a variety of reasons, many divorcees have reported that if they had it to do over they would not have gotten divorced. Many reach the decision to break up their marriages rather suddenly and fail to consider many factors which have an important bearing on their future. For example, one woman was so sick of the miserable marriage she had been enduring that one day she decided she had had all she could take. She took her baby and walked out, leaving everything behind—home, furniture, and economic security. She wanted no part of any of it any more. Her husband had inherited a small fortune, enough that he did not really have to work. The woman was so anxious to end her unhappy marriage, however, that it never occurred to her that she had any right or responsibility to try to take any of their property or his income. Her husband, through her attorney's efforts, did make a commitment to provide child support, and for some years did so faithfully. After a few years, however, he ran through most of his inheritance by bad business ventures, and the payments stopped coming for a time. Later they were renewed on a percentage basis. She would have been better off economically if she had petitioned the court through her attorney for a greater share of her former husband's financial resources. This sort of tragedy is not uncommon for men or women because sometimes the husband is so desperate to get out of the marriage that he agrees hastily to "give her whatever she wants" and winds up in an economic trap for years to come.

Often, in the midst of anger and hostility toward each other, both the husband and the wife will lose sight of a number of things they need to

56

consider as calmly and as objectively as possible. For example they may lose sight of what they are doing to themselves and to each other that they will later regret, like creating guilt feelings by doing and saying things that are really uncharacteristic of either husband or wife. For another example, in the midst of the passions of the moment, husbands and wives may lose sight of the effects of what they say or do on the children and the possibility of their surviving the trauma of marital breakup with emotional balance.

It is the purpose of this chapter to call attention to several types of factors that both the husband and the wife should consider in the process of divorce.

Legal Factors

One of the first questions one may face once the decision for divorce has been made is whether to get a lawyer. Until recently in most states, a lawyer was almost always a necessity because of the legal requirement that legal fault be established on the part of one or both partners to justify the breakup of the marriage. Beginning in 1969, when the first no-fault divorce legislation was passed by the state of California, this requirement has been removed from many state laws, and the securing of a divorce has been somewhat simplified. The result is that in some cases a "do it yourself divorce" is a real possibility. The awareness of the no-fault divorce law, however, may obscure the fact that many complicated laws are still on the books in many states and that choosing the simple no-fault and "do it yourself" divorce is very risky. The "do it yourself" procedure may be justified only under two circumstances. The first is where you are absolutely sure of the procedure. The second is where there are no children and no property involved. In all circumstances, one will do well to consider the saying that is common among lawyers: "a lawyer who represents himself in court has a fool for a client." If this saying suggests that a lawyer needs legal representation in court, it should be obvious that a nonlawyer needs it more. Eisler is right when she suggests that, if you have any doubt about whether to secure an attorney, it is best at least to talk to one.[1]

How do you choose a lawyer, and what kind should you choose? I would suggest that you consider several factors about available lawyers which can be learned by inquiring among friends and by interviewing the lawyers themselves. The latter may cost money since some lawyers charge small fees for consultation. Ask about that. It is worth finding out. First, you should consider the estimated cost suggested by the attorney. Most attorneys charge an hourly rate, but it may be very unwise to choose the one with the lowest rate. Even though in many areas the rate is uniform, the costs can vary widely. Second, you should consider the efficiency of the attorney. Some attorneys who are very competent work more slowly than others and the resulting differences in costs among attorney's fees is sometimes amazing. I have known of instances where lawyers have privately admitted that some of their colleagues were overpricing their own services because of their inefficiency. Sometimes this problem is made unavoidable by clients who waste much of the lawyer's time by forcing him to spend hours serving as a personal and psychological counselor, which may not require legal knowledge at all. An attorney may endure such a process to avoid offending you. Some problems you have may be better told to a minister who probably will make no charge at all. When you consult an attorney, have your facts and purposes clear in your mind in order to make the most efficient use of your time and that of the attorney. It may save you money. It must be added, however, that thoroughness is also a part of efficiency and that sometimes quick action may not be the wisest. Even the best attorney needs time to work on a case.

Third, you should consider the attorney's reputation for fairness to both men and women. Sheresky and Mannes claim that too many attorneys for husbands judge their success by how little the husband winds up paying his ex-wife and the children. Too many attorneys for wives judge their success by how much they can get from the husband for the wife.[2] Often one partner in the marriage breakup may decide that, since both the husband and the wife are agreed on getting a divorce, there is no point in hiring two attorneys and will assume that one lawyer can represent both persons. Unless the couple has agreed on every detail, this approach is risky. The legal system is based on the premise that an attorney usually represents one client, and some naive husbands and wives have been victimized by the apparent bias of the attorney who is really doing only what he was employed to do. Whoever pays the lawyer is likely to have the advantage.

Sheresky and Mannes also say that some lawyers who are very effective in representing husbands are very poor at representing wives.[3] This observation is important and ought to be considered in choosing an attorney. Lawyers are human. Learn to recognize one who may be more likely to be fair.

Finally, look for an attorney who is experienced in divorce law and divorce procedure. Law has now become highly complicated and specialized, so that no lawyer can be expert and efficient in all types of law. One who is experienced in handling divorce cases can be more efficient and less costly than others.

Closely related to the question of choosing a lawyer is the legal question of property. Laws governing the property that is involved in a marriage are complicated even in those states with no-fault divorce. These laws govern the rights of the husband, the wife, and the children, but often flexibility is allowed in the implementation of these laws by the agreement signed by the husband and the wife in the divorce decree. As I have suggested earlier, very often marital partners sign these agreements without much awareness of their consequences. A person in the process of getting a divorce needs to be as aware as possible of both the immediate and long-term consequences of a particular property settlement. Each one needs to consider the certainties and the uncertainties of securing future changes in the arrangements. You do well to inquire about the legal possibilities pertaining to every aspect of the economics and property involved in your past life together and the effects this past life might have on your future security. For example, you should inquire about what the law says about division of present property and sharing in future income which results from the life you have had together. This matter is of urgency because as Eisler says the laws governing property in marital disputes in many states are neither clear nor consistent.[4] You need to know what property is held, in whose name, and how divorce law affects these questions. In questions of property settlements, the services of an attorney is usually an absolute necessity.

Closely related to the legal question of property are the questions of child support, alimony, visitation rights, taxes, medical bills, insurance, wills, and trusts, and educational expenses. Questions about these factors are usually part of the legal contract that involves property settlements and that make up the divorce decree. When you sign the divorce agreement, you are agreeing to a group of complicated decisions that may affect your life for years to come and that cannot be easily undone. Indeed in many instances they may not be undone at all. You do well to learn all you can about the laws governing these matters before you consult an attorney. Such information is often obtainable at a public library or through university or community college extension courses. Obtaining as much of this information on your own as possible is not a substitute for the services of your lawyer. It may help you in dealing with the lawyer in two ways however. First, it can help you to understand what the lawyer explains to you. Despite an attorney's best efforts, many clients sign statements they do not fully understand and later regret. Second, it can save your time with the attorney and, therefore, save you money. However, do not suppress important questions to save time. Do not hesitate to ask, for example, under what circumstances you may refuse visitation rights to your former mate. Such questions may save you much grief in the future.

It is particularly important to recognize that, although the children of divorcees are not referred to as property since they often have no legal standing before the courts, they are virtually treated as property. Although there are laws that govern child custody, the courts will often honor whatever agreements the parents may reach. It is imperative that whatever agreement is reached be very clear to everyone involved, for once the agreement is signed, child custody is hard to change.

Your preparation for consulting a lawyer may do well to include familiarizing yourself with the most common types of divorces and deciding which type fits your situation. First is the simple divorce involving no children and little or no property where both partners want the divorce. A divorce of this type is usually obtainable very quickly, and the cost is low. A second type is divorce by default. This type describes a situation where one partner has deserted the family and has nothing to do with the proceedings. Sometimes this kind of divorce can be very simple, quick, and economical, with a judge deciding the terms. A third type, sometimes called a no-fault divorce, is a divorce in which the couple agrees that there should be a divorce, divide up the property, and make decisions about the children. Usually, they sign an agreement in the presence of their attorney or attorneys before going to court. The final type of divorce is a contested divorce, where one partner wants it and the other does not and tries to prove that there are no grounds. A judge decides the validity of their claims.

In all these types that involve both partners in the proceedings, an agreement is usually signed. It is urgent that both partners have a clear understanding of the agreement. Much grief results from failures in communication even when the agreement is in writing.[5]

Moral Considerations

In the heat of conflict over the dissolution of the marriage, very often either or both marital partners will set aside moral considerations and become obsessed with all the revenge that the law will allow. The law is often an excellent guide to what is fair and is properly intended to reduce or avoid flagrant moral offenses. However, it is often too much to expect of the law to assume that whatever is legal is, therefore, moral and ethical. There are some very important ethical questions which should be considered independently of what the law requires and allows, and these questions should be considered in reflecting on the agreements that are signed. In addition they are important because of their bearing on other decisions not set forth in the agreement. They are particularly important to those who are committed to the Christian faith and to the values of the Judeo-Christian tradition.

The first of these ethical questions is, What would be the best way to get out of the marriage with the least injury to your mate? You need to remember that no matter what he (or she) has done, he (or she) is a person for whom Christ died. You need to remember that revenge has no place in the life of a Christian and that, while Nietzsche may have a point when he said that a little revenge is sweet, I maintain that in the long run revenge is bad for anyone. Your mate is a person who needs forgiveness and the opportunity to rebuild a life as you do. You should consider the need and the right of your mate to live a decent life without being deprived of the necessities or the satisfactions that accompany a decent life. You need also to recognize that the obligations you owe may require a simpler life-style for you; for often after a divorce, there is a genuine economic loss for both the husband and the wife. All this means that the prime question should not be, How much can I get from the divorce settlement? but What would be fair for everyone involved? Sometimes the law is helpful in deciding what is fair, but not always. The best-adjusted divorcees I have met have been those who never lost concern for the well-being of their former mates.

A second ethical question has to do with your responsibility for your own well-being. How you are going to live after the marriage is dissolved? The court is not likely to resolve that question. You need to face seriously your possibilities and your responsibilities. It is not only not wrong to recognize the need for looking out for yourself but also it is your responsibility. Looking out for yourself, however, means not getting all you can and giving as little as you can, but it means developing a balanced view of your rights and responsibilities. Fundamental to this problem is the recognition of the degree to which the incurring of debts created in the marriage, for example, reflect shared responsibilities. The same question needs to be considered in regard to income and credit cards.

Closely related to both these ethical questions of the well-being of your mate and your own well-being is the question of your responsibility for the children. How are they to be cared for? What is your responsibility? What factors will affect your ability to bear your responsibilities in the future? You have a responsibility not only to carry your part of the load in the present but also to make your plans so that you will still be able to carry them out in the future. Sometimes after the dissolution of the marriage, the ex-husband or ex-wife will plan how legally to get out of responsibility in the future. It is often possible, though difficult, to get legal agreements changed. Eisler gives examples of how this sort of thing occurs.[6]

My argument is that, if you have the right sense of responsibility, your prime concern will be to plan your life and activities in such a way as to provide for the well-being of the children and to cooperate with your ex-mate in whatever ways are necessary to achieve that end. You need to remember that, at best, divorce is a traumatic experience for the children, and some authorities claim none of them ever get over it. I am convinced that many of them never get over it. The children of divorce whom I have observed who adjust best are the children of those parents who have genuinely accepted their mutual responsibility for the economic, spiritual, and emotional well-being of the children. They accepted that mutual responsibility because they decided early in the process of divorce that their mutual responsibility for the economic, emotional, and spiritual well-being of their children did not end when the marriage ended. The children of such responsible parents still find the acceptance of divorce hard, but they know they still have both parents, and that knowledge is no small comfort to them.

Genuine dialogue with the children is extremely important. Sometimes arrangements are made by the parents, close relatives, and/or social agencies for the care of the children without much genuine communication with the children. Because the children often consider themselves to be the cause of the divorce, they often will try to accept any arrangement for their keeping, however destructive it may be. However, another reaction from children may be negative and destructive, as the suicide of a teenager who was sent to live with his grandmother when his parents divorced. I am confident that if the parents had had any notion of the damage that was being done to him by the way the family was split up, they would have tried to find some other way. Of course, none of us can always know the full consequences that our decisions made in a crisis may have, but we should learn to calculate them as best we can.

Finally, you should consider the importance of guarding your own moral life during and following the process of the divorce. Often the divorce is a shattering experience to a moral person who has genuinely tried to do everything right. Now you may be thinking, *What did it get me?* You may be tempted, therefore, to ignore your moral ideals, not realizing that the underlying driving force which almost compels you to do so is not your moral scruples or the loss of them, but the desire for revenge against your mate—a desire you would not approve at your best. You need to remember, therefore, that the process of getting a divorce may be a time of moral testing. Failure to keep your moral stability, failing the moral testing, can end in greater despair than the despair over the breakup of the marriage itself. Decide not only to continue to be the moral person you were but also to become a better person than you were. The trauma of divorce is likely either to make you better or worse than you were before. Which it is, is up to you.

Spiritual Problems

I have written elsewhere about the problem divorcees encounter some times among church people who tend to regard them as second-class citizens and how divorcees might deal with that problem. Here I wish to describe some other spiritual problems because the shock of divorce sometimes places a serious strain on one's faith. You may be tempted to blame God for the divorce, especially if you began your marriage on what you thought was a solid spiritual basis and, when the problems developed, you prayed for help in saving the marriage. Then it appeared that no help came. You must remember that God gives us freedom and that, even with the help of God, a strong marriage requires the cooperation of two persons. If even one partner is unwilling to cooperate in making a marriage work, the marriage cannot be saved.

One man got married shortly after high school to his high school sweetheart and then entered the military service. The couple was separated from each other for long periods of time. While in the service, he said later, he prayed for his wife to be faithful to him. To his dismay he came home to find that she had been unfaithful. She seemed genuinely sorry. While he seemed willing to forgive her, the main object of his resentment was God. He did not seem to understand the freedom we have. Often one's hostility toward one's former mate is projected on God, and this creates a very serious spiritual problem which can damage the spiritual and emotional life of the individual. To be free spiritually from a divorce, one must both forgive and be forgiven for whatever wrongs were involved in the breakup of the marriage. To face one's own responsibility for the breakup of the marriage is good, as stated earlier, but to attempt to fix blame is a risky affair because it easily generates new hostility to one's former mate, to God, or to both.

A second spiritual problem has to do with the spiritual life of the children. Often the breakup of a marriage is accompanied by a break with the church, not a deliberate break, but a break, nonetheless. The same concern for the economic well-being of the former mate and the children which was recommended earlier is needed for the spiritual well-being of one's former mate and the children as well. The husband and the wife will do well to discuss this matter calmly, for the children of divorce need the comfort, support, and ministry of the church more than ever. Often where there are religious differences between the husband and the wife, this can be a real problem. The usual result of such differences is that the child will have no connection with the church at all. The parents will do well to set aside some of their religious differences insofar as they are related to the child. While it may be confusing to the child to be taken to two different churches, according to which parent is in charge, it might be less damaging to the spiritual growth of the child than to have no relation to any church at all. A proper concern for the spiritual life of the child is part of the responsibility the parents continue to share even after the marriage is broken.

Finally, it is important to continue one's relationship to the Christian community, the church. When two partners breaking up their marriage belong to the same church and continue to live in the same area, this can be a problem. Both may feel too embarrassed to continue worshiping in the same place with one's former mate. Awareness of the possibility of gossip can be distressing. However, where both members have close ties in the church, to stay with the same church may be, in some cases, the very best thing. Emotional and spiritual support from old friends in the church can be very comforting. Moreover divorcees need the church more than ever. The questions of what to say to old friends and how to tell them are difficult but not impossible. The simplest response is a simple brief declaration of the truth.

In recent years, the attitude of many church people and churches toward divorce and the divorcee have changed substantially. The divorced person may be surprised what support can be had in the church. One can grow through a crisis, and one who has grown through the crisis of divorce can be the means by which others grow from other crises. The reason is that we grow in part through suffering. In the process of divorce and after the divorce, some counseling with a minister who is knowledgeable and understanding can help this process of growth. Divorce can be a tragedy which blights the rest of one's life, or it can be the door to new growth. Spiritual counsel from a qualified person and a good relationship to a healthy church can help in making the experience of divorce a growth experience.

Notes

1. Riane Tennenhaus Eisler, *Dissolution: No Fault Divorce, Marriage and the Future of Women* (New York: McGraw-Hill, 1977) p. 224.
2. Norman Sheresky and Mary Mannes, *Uncoupling: The Art of Coming Apart* (New York: The Viking Press, 1972), p. x.
3. Ibid., p. 44.
4. Eisler, p. 34.
5. Carol Kleiman, "Split Decisions," *Orlando Sentinel Star,* November 12, 1981.
6. Eisler, pp. 24 *ff.*

5
Dealing with the Aftermath: Feelings and Facts

In his book *Til Divorce Do Us Part,* R. Lofton Hudson calls divorce the funeral of a dead marriage.[1] While he gives some attention to the subject of this chapter, the prime concern of Hudson's book lies elsewhere. Assuming that Hudson is right in his description of divorce, the questions asked in this chapter are, What do you do after the funeral? What will you do with the corpse? Your divorce may be a tragedy in your eyes and in the eyes of many of your friends; but if so, it is a tragedy you must learn to accept and help your friends to accept. A few days before I wrote these lines a former student of mine came by with her husband for a visit and reported their shock in learning of the recent divorce of another young couple they had planned to visit. They were in a state of grief with a variety of confused emotions over the discovery. In many cases, the couple which is getting a divorce are experiencing far more profound grief and confusion in their emotions than their friends could ever imagine. This leads to my first answer to the question about what you do after the funeral of a dead marriage.

Facing and Accepting the Tragedy

With divorce comes a flood of emotions in many ways similar to those which occur when a mate dies. In some ways I suspect that the grief of the newly divorced may be more painful than that of the one who has lost a marital partner through death. One of the first things the divorcee has to do is to face and accept the tragedy with all the flood of emotions that are involved. The divorcee must accept these feelings as a part of his or her humanity. Most of these feelings are very normal, and your experience of them is a sign of emotional health. First among the feelings which are normal and common is the feeling of hostility to one's mate. One tends easily to project all or most of the blame for the marriage failure on the other person. In many instances, the hostility is at least understandable. Often in the process of marriage dissolution, two people who have loved each other deeply find themselves hurting each other and feeling the horrible stinging pain of being hurt by one they loved. The hurt individuals may feel betrayed and find it very difficult to forgive. Sometimes the hostility is repressed, and the individual does not admit the truth even though the hostility is there. Rationalizations, such as "I do not hate him, but I resent the way he has treated me," may be ways of avoiding the truth. Often hostility and resentment are the same, and they becloud the emotions of the bereaved divorcee. When hostility is present, it needs to be faced and handled appropriately. The appropriate way to handle it is to give it up by forgiving the ex-partner to whom it has been directed. The partner needs to be forgiven because almost invariably, in the process of the marriage breakup, one says and does things and inflicts damage on others that cannot be undone, that cannot be corrected. The only way to freedom is forgiveness.

A second emotional feeling which follows divorce is guilt and self-condemnation. Like hostility, guilt feelings may be on the surface or in the depths of the emotions and, therefore, lie unacknowledged, but they are usually there. And they, like the feelings of hostility, need to be brought to the surface. These feelings of guilt, moreover, may or may not represent an accurate appraisal of reality, but they still need to be faced. Often divorcees carry loads of guilt all out of proportion to reality and may need to be told by caring counselors who have a more objective view of the situations to stop the process of self-condemnation. This problem will be addressed in more detail in a later chapter, but here we must observe that the parents may contribute to the guilt feelings of the children by their own self-condemnation. The children may think, *If our parents who are surely better than we are, feel guilty, then surely we are more guilty than they are.* This may be the reason children of divorce often blame themselves for their parents' divorces. Often, however, as we have suggested above, the feeling of guilt for divorcees is an accurate expression of a reality. One feels guilty because one is guilty, and often the expression of hostility toward the mate is, in part at least, an attempt to cover up the painful reality of one's own guilt. Face the facts. In marriage and out of marriage, we have all sinned, we are all guilty, and we all need forgiveness. We need forgiveness in part because we have said and done things we cannot undo and because we have violated God's intentions for us. Part of what divorcees need to see is that the guilt and the hostility they feel may be more acute at the time for them than for others, they are part of what is common to all of us. The good news of the gospel is that there is forgiveness available to all of us in Jesus Christ.

A third feeling that needs to be faced is the tendency to self-pity. The newly divorced often feel cheated and are tempted to indulge in self-pity. This feeling is understandable, for often the divorcee has been cheated out of something that was very precious. The temptation to indulge in self-pity is one which is common to most of us. There is, indeed, a certain kind of pleasure we derive from it. But like some other pleasures, if we indulge in it too long, it tends to turn sour and become morbid. The danger is real that the divorcee will become trapped in morbid indulgence in self-pity. Therefore, the divorcee must not allow the feeling of self-pity to become a habit. Symptomatic of the danger of morbidity is the tendency to continue the obsession with one's divorce. Mary Ann Singleton suggests that this obsession is one of the stages through which one goes. The divorcee is tempted to latch on to everyone she (or he) sees and say, "Let me tell you about my divorce." Singleton says this temptation usually lasts about a year.[2] I suggest that within this period some indulgence in self-pity is human and normal. If it continues, however, it is morbid and symptomatic of serious unresolved problems. Finally, the feeling of general anxiety often overwhelms the divorcee. Anxiety and depression go hand in hand.

Another common experience of the newly divorced, and often the most painful of all, is the acute feeling of loneliness. Sometimes it not only lingers but also becomes more acute after some of the other emotions mentioned above have been brought under control. In some ways, moreover, the failure to deal creatively with the problem of loneliness may turn out to be the most costly tragedy in the whole divorce experience. The reason is dramatically indicated in some recent studies that seem to indicate that being alone can be dangerous to physical, psychological, and emotional health. One such study was reported many years ago by Ashley Montagu at Rutgers, who observed that children in foundling homes died for no apparent cause. Studies of their deaths concluded the reason was that they were not given love and personal affection.[3] Left alone without human affection, even though given all the usual physical needs, children die.

So do adults, according to James J. Lynch, professor at the School of Medicine at the University of Maryland. He reports on a study begun in 1948 in the small town of Framington, Massachusetts, by joint efforts of the U.S. government and a group of medical scientists to determine the cause or risk factors in one of the leading causes of death in the United States, namely heart disease. They discovered a number of factors that are now well known and brought new emphasis on diet and exercise as means of preventing heart disease.

Dr. Lynch, however, has noted an additional risk factor which was implicitly documented in the studies, but not noticed by others. That risk factor was loneliness. He concluded that, unless we learn to deal creatively with the problem of loneliness, we are likely to die earlier than we otherwise would. He offers some concrete evidence that suggests that those who live alone experience more physical illness and die younger than those who live with other people. He points out that the death rate among singles and the widowed is higher than it is among those who are still married. The fundamental problem in divorce and widowhood is the breakdown in dialogue, which is necessary to life. In other words, if you do not deal with loneliness creatively, it can kill you.[4]

While we must make a distinction between loneliness and being alone, which Lynch never quite makes, we must acknowledge the importance of his study. I would argue that it is not the fact of being alone itself that results in the evidence that Lynch cites. Rather, he can cite the evidence he does for his conclusions simply because most people do not learn to handle the problem of loneliness creatively. While the problem of loneliness, like the other experiences which have been mentioned, is not unique to divorcees, it is obviously a special problem for them. Many divorcees say they could not have imagined how painful the loneliness would be. One woman, still dominated by hostility toward her ex-husband, admitted that while she still hated him she missed him terribly. She was learning to be honest. The loneliness is so powerful for some that they feel driven to take drastic measures in dealing with it, measures which are not creative. One example is the temptation to indulge in sexual experimentation as an effort to overcome the loneliness. Lynch correctly observes that sexual promiscuity is one of several traps which are simply efforts to deny the problem.[5]

There are more creative ways of dealing with this potentially dangerous problem of loneliness. First, the divorcee should face the fact that loneliness, like the other emotional feelings, is a normal and universal problem. It is a reality to be recognized and accepted. Jesus was lonely. He felt abandoned by God and man (Luke 23:27-53), but he not only recognized loneliness but also made creative efforts to deal with it. The divorcee should respond to the problem of loneliness the same way Jesus did. Let the divorcee take a good look at his (or her) personal relationships. Jesus began to bridge the gap by praying for forgiveness for those who were estranged from him. Forgiveness will help the divorcee to bridge the gap of loneliness also.

A second creative way to deal with the problem of loneliness is to take a good look at yourself. Jeremiah in the Old Testament knew the feeling of loneliness, as did Jesus, Paul, and Timothy in the New Testament. Each of these great biblical personalities may have found being alone a painful experience. But for them, being alone was also a constructive experience in which they grew because they got to know themselves better. Learning to use being alone as an opportunity to get to know oneself is an important part of becoming a mature person. When one learns how to handle being alone with creativity, one is then better prepared to be in the company of others. Dietrich Bonhoeffer made this point well in *Life Together*. His creative response to the loneliness of prison life has resulted in a rich intellectual and theological dialogue which can be entered into by today's Christians who read his writings.[6]

A third way of dealing with the problem of loneliness is crying out to others for help. Again, Jesus acknowledged his need for others. On the cross, he cried, "I thirst." Often we suffer in our loneliness because our vain pride keeps us from asking for help when it is available. Often others would share our loneliness and help us to overcome it if only we would give them a chance. Beware, however, of those who exploit the loneliness of others to their advantage. One of the safest places to raise your cry is in the context of the church.

Fourth, the divorcee can deal with the problem of loneliness by making plans that involve others. Reach out to them. Find ways to invest your life in service to and with others. It is true that many divorcees are reluctant to reach out to others because they fear rejection. Sometimes these fears are well founded because the divorcees have been ostracized by some of their former friends. However, Ira Tanner has a point when he argues that loneliness results more from our fear of loving than from the reality of being rejected. Moreover, he says that the sad truth is that the lonely person who fears reaching out because of the possibility of rejection is lonelier than ever because of hesitation.[7] When we learn to love and reach out expecting nothing, we will be delighted when we evoke a response and the feeling of loneliness may vanish.

A fifth way of dealing with the problem of loneliness is to recognize that you are really never alone (Jer. 15:15-21; Matt. 28:19-20). Jeremiah felt alone, but God reminded him that he was not really abandoned. Neither is the divorcee. The divorcee may be abandoned or rejected by former friends or in some cases even by the church, but never by God.

To deal with loneliness creatively, the divorcee also needs to repent of sin. All of us have sinned and loneliness is sometimes a symptom of rebellion against God. It was for the prophet Jeremiah, and it may be for us as well. Loneliness may result from the distance we create between ourselves and God when we rebel against his will for our lives.

Finally, the divorcee may feel helpless and listless, unwilling or unable to make some fundamental decisions that need to be made. In general terms, all these emotional reactions are normal and should be accepted as part of one's humanity. At the same time, they should not be allowed to continue to dominate one.

Analyzing the Reasons for the Divorce

In the aftermath of a divorce, it is also important for the divorcee to spend some time reflecting on the reasons for the divorce. Although the subjective involvement of the divorcee may make this very difficult and sometimes impossible to do with accuracy, it is important to try. Something may be learned that can help one in the future. Divorce can be a tragic blight for the rest of your life or it can be a door to new life and growth. For some at least, in order for it to be a means to new growth, an understanding of the dynamics of the process that broke up the marriage is necessary. One of the prime tests of maturity is the ability to learn from one's mistakes, and we cannot learn from mistakes if we do not recognize them. Addeo makes this general point effectively.[8] People get divorced for a variety of reasons. Some divorce perhaps because it is the style. Others break up their marriages because they discover that keeping a marriage together requires a good deal of work and they are not willing to work at it. Still others divorce because they have serious personality problems. For a person with personality problems, the divorce is viewed as the solution to the personality problems. This is a point made well many years ago by Edmund Bergler in *Divorce Won't Help*.[9] A person with a personality problem may break up his (or her) marriage to get out of the problem, when in fact the problem goes with the individual. Such a person, unwilling to face the problem, easily forms the habit of projecting the problem on the other person in the partnership. This kind of person marries and divorces partners frequently. Sometimes it may be necessary to get out of a marriage, but if you fail to learn from your mistakes and recognize the problem you have which contributed to the failure of the marriage, you are likely to repeat your mistakes. Counseling may be required. Several divorcees with whom I have counseled have told me all divorcees should have counseling. I do not think I agree that all should, but I am confident that many would profit from it.

Others divorce because they find their marriage an impossibility where two people are in the process of hurting themselves and each other and where growth for either partner is impossible. Such persons often decide that some distance must be established before any objective appraisal of one's own problem or the problem in the relationship can be made. Of course, we must recognize that sometimes even with the help of a counselor it may be impossible to discover all the reasons a marriage turned sour. Sometimes the factors are too varied and complex. The point is that we are better prepared for the future if we learn what we can from our past.

Avoiding Emotional Traps

In addition to the primary emotions discussed at the beginning of this chapter, a number of other emotional traps may continue to threaten one's future growth after control over the primary emotions has been gained. These emotional traps may have some roots in unresolved problems. They may have other roots in some of the romantic notions perpetuated in society. Still other roots may be found in peer pressure groups created by other divorcees who have failed to learn the lesson dealt with in the preceding section. They may be the cynics who freely advise the newly divorced. Divorcees and those who befriend them need to be aware of these traps.

I am indebted to Krantzler for his excellent description of these traps. The first of these emotional traps is the temptation to make broad generalizations about all divorcees. They are not all alike. Despite some general characteristics that are common to some, when considered in detail, every divorce and every divorcee is unique. Outsiders judging divorcees often err here. Many divorcees complain of this error with justification.[10]

A second emotional trap may be the temptation to conclude too hastily that one has learned the secret about the marriage-divorce problem. This trap may be an expansion of the one just mentioned, as it may take varied forms with each individual. The hasty conclusions may have a wide range. For example, the woman may conclude: "That's the way men are. They are only interested in one thing—sex." Or the man may say, "That's the way women are, only interested in one thing—money." One man who had been married three times and was living with first one woman and then another told me: "I have been a millionaire three times, and one woman ruined me." I doubt it. Another example would be a person who has been hurt so badly that she concludes that marriage is a big pain in the neck. Injured by love, she may be afraid to love again because to her love is pain. The problem with this particular approach is that the fear of loving which grows out of it is a far more destructive trap.

Another example of a hasty conclusion is the developing or unreal expectations on the positive side. One may say: "Well I messed up this marriage, but the next one will be perfect." Such a person may be setting himself or herself up for very bitter disillusionment. Still another hasty conclusion may be the tendency to fix the blame too easily and simply. As a matter of fact, despite my earlier counsel about analyzing the causes for the failure of the marriage, the attempt to fix the blame is a dangerous response, for it can easily keep alive or revive the hostility.

A third emotional trap is the tendency to spend too much time thinking about oneself. Self-examination is a good thing, but there is a difference between creative self-examination and preoccupation with self. The strange paradox is that time spent alone by the divorcee can bring new insights into personal problems, or it can destroy the possibility of communication with others. One can isolate oneself too much.

A fourth emotional trap is the temptation to flee from oneself by keeping so busy that there is no time at all for reflection. This can be a trap by which one escapes some needed self-confrontation which we have mentioned.

A fifth emotional trap is closely related to the fourth. It is the temptation not only to continue one's dependency but also to accentuate it. This temptation to continue one's psychological and emotional dependency relationship takes either or both of two forms. First, it may take the form of continued dependence on one's mate. One divorced friend still thinks of herself as married. Even though she has been divorced for some time, attends church conferences for singles, and even leads a singles group, she says she does not think of herself as a single. Here may be the yearning of the half person about which Krantzler has spoken.[11] One member of my church thirty years ago persisted in thinking his wife would return to him four years after their divorce when it seemed obvious to everyone else that it would never happen.

A second example of the temptation to continue some kind of dependency relationship which is no longer practical is the temptation to over-identify with one's children. This is an important point, but it is one that can be misunderstood. An example of the point I wish to make is the case of a woman who freed herself from her dependency relationship with her husband by transferring it to her children. To give extra attention to the children of divorce is normal and important. The danger is that the normal and even necessary concern for the children by mother or father can easily develop into a domination of the children. Sometimes such a parent is never able to give the children the psychological freedom they need to become their own unique selves. The parent may easily become so obsessed with what she (or he) thinks is living for the children, when in really the parent's own self-identity becomes totally tied up with being a parent. This is especially a threat to the mother who, more often than not, is left with the responsibility of caring for the children. This kind of dependency relation may lead to at least two unfortunate consequences. First, when the children leave home to be on their own, the dependent parent may feel abandoned and become embittered, cynical, and hostile toward the children. Second, the parent may contribute to guilt feelings in children who often feel responsible for the separation and divorce of their parents. For the emotional health of both parents, while responsibility for the continued care of the children is very important, it is equally important that the identity of the parent not become attached exclusively to the relationship with the children. Those who come to think of their children primarily as extensions of their own selfhood are hurting themselves and the children. And children who accept the dependency relationship are sowing seeds of serious emotional insecurity that will be apparent when they lose the dependent parent.

Becoming a Whole Person Again

Often marriage does involve the blending of two personalities in such a way that the loss of the unity by divorce or death results in the feeling of being half a person. A widowed friend told me some time ago that, after the death of her husband to whom she had been happily married for many years, she had to learn to think as an individual for the first time in many years. Many divorcees have the same problem. In fact, for many divorcees the problem may be worse because the divorcee's mate is often still somewhere around. According to research reported by Robert S. Weiss, many divorcees still feel a bond toward their former mate even after a new relationship has been established with another person.[12] Two women I met at a singles conference illustrated this problem in their own experiences. I had met each of them at a similar conference the year before. Within a year's time, both of them had been remarried and divorced again. They both realized after our conference that they had remarried before they were free from the previous marital bond.

Divorcees need to realize that regardless of whether or not remarriage is to be considered in the future, if they want to be truly free, they have to dissolve the emotional bonds with their former mates and become whole persons again. This need does not require forgetting one's mate or even breaking all contact with the former partner, but it does require that the psychological relationship of dependency be broken.

On the positive side, becoming a whole person again means developing a new sense of self-identity. Achieving this goal requires some fundamental decisions about one's own selfhood. The first of these decisions is self-acceptance. The divorcee needs to decide not to indulge in the temptation of self-pity which we mentioned at the beginning of this chapter. Also one must decide not to accept the identity which, in some cases, will be thrust upon one by one's peers or by the social group or groups in which one moves. Some of you will find yourselves in situations where you think you are made to feel like second-class citizens. Numerous divorcees have told me that church people make them feel so. I argue, however, that no one can make you feel like a second-class citizen. You may be right in your perception of how you are regarded, but you do not have to accept their classification of you. In fact you should not accept it, for you are no more a failure as a person because of your marriage failure than anyone else. In some ways we all fail. Part of what is involved in being a whole person is being able to buck peer pressure and discover personal identity.

In some cases, a divorcee may have to develop a whole new set of friends, as an alcoholic does. In Alcoholics Anonymous, the alcoholic becomes a part of a new set of peers who help him to be free to be himself and to accept himself. They help the alcoholic to do this by becoming a loving, caring community whose acceptance of the newcomer is unconditional. You may say, "But I am not an alcoholic. Where can I find such a community for divorcees?" I answer that you should begin by making a fundamental decision that will prepare you for participation in such a community. That fundamental decision is for self-acceptance.

The good news of the Christian message is that in Jesus Christ you are accepted. The theological ground for your self-acceptance is in the doctrine of justification by faith. Faith means, among other things, the courage to believe that you are accepted before God because of what Jesus Christ has done for you, even though you know yourself to be unacceptable. The Christian message to you is that in his Son Jesus Christ, God has loved you with an everlasting and unconditional love. It is that God has decided that you are a lovable person. And if God considers you a lovable person and others do not, they have a problem. Believe the good news of the gospel. Forget the past. You may have to think of yourself as acceptable again.

Now you may say, "But what if my friends do not think of me as acceptable?" I answer that you must decide that, as you have been accepted unconditionally, you must accept your judgmental friends without conditions. If they cannot accept your acceptance, their problem may be worse than yours. Divorcees sometimes feel that the world has mistreated them and often their small part of it has. Often they are shut out by former friends. On occasion, these friends include fellow church members and the temptation to be hostile toward all these people who have failed you is understandable. However, you need to realize that the response of hostility will only widen the gap that needs to be closed. In accepting yourself and others, you will not only move toward becoming a whole person again but also you will be helping others to move in the same direction.

The divorcee needs to understand that the changed relationship with former friends does not always reflect hostility and rejection by those friends. Often it reflects confusion and uncertainty. Many people are so shocked at the divorce of friends whose marriage seemed solid that they do not know how to relate to their former friends. Just before I wrote this chapter I received a visit from a former student who reported that she simply did not know what to say when close friends of hers told her they were getting a divorce. It is quite possible that her shock was so obvious to her friends that it was taken as rejection.

While many divorcees have felt rejection in the church, others have found acceptance and warm support here. Fortunately, in recent years, many church people have softened their attitudes toward divorcees, including those who are remarried. This leads me to an important suggestion: to become a whole person and to deal with the painful aftermath of divorce, I recommend that the divorcee find a useful place of service in the church and community. Numerous opportunities for church and community service exist in every community, and not only will the divorcee help to avoid boredom and self-pity by becoming involved in such service but also in the midst of such service a new sense of self-identity may develop. Sometimes, changing jobs helps this process. A friend whose marriage failure inflicted a devastating blow to her self-confidence gradually recovered her self-image as she became involved in the life of a caring Sunday School teacher and church. Later she changed jobs and now is a partner in a successful public relations and advertising business and is really a new person.

Consider Your Advantages

When you are divorced, you can either reflect on your misfortunes and meditate on how you have been cheated, or you can take account of your possibilities and advantages. You probably could be a lot worse off. Think, for example, of what you still have that others do not. If you have health, youth, a job, a home, an education, children, any or all of these, you have something for which to be thankful. Did you have something that was precious that you have now lost? You can either indulge in self-pity or you can give thanks that you had it. There may be others who have never had it. Your divorce may provide an opportunity to do something you have long wanted to do and have been unable to accomplish. Many have discovered that, while they did not get divorced for this purpose, divorce made possible the pursuing of careers that brought far more satisfactions than unhappy marriages.

A University of Florida professor has argued that being divorced has great advantages over being widowed, especially in the competition for companionship with the opposite sex. Some women who have been both divorced and widowed have also concluded that most men would rather compete with a live competitor than a dead one. Often a man who has been divorced is trying to forget a rejected mate and finds it easy to do so, while one whose mate is dead may idealize the departed mate and compare any new prospects with her. Thus a divorcee can be told, Cheer up. You could be a widow, and that could be worse than being a divorcee. Count your advantages, consider your possibilities, and make plans to make the most of them.[13]

Some Words to Friends of the Divorcee

Despite their good intentions and sometimes even their best efforts, friends and/or counselors of the divorcee often fail them. They usually do not mean to do so, and sometimes the thing they think might help their friend most, hurts the most. While the suggestions I am going to make may not apply equally to every divorcee, they will apply to many, and the friend or counselor of the divorcee should develop a sensitivity to the unique needs of each friend.

First, I would suggest that your friends should not be shut out of your life because of their divorce. This problem is a common complaint of divorcees. I have talked with many divorcees and some friends of divorcees about this problem, and I have concluded that in many instances the friends of the divorced person do not intend to convey the feeling that comes across to the divorcee. They simply do not know how to handle the problem of a continued relationship. The central problem for the friends appears to be the fear of offending one of the divorced couple by excluding him while inviting her to a social function. At the same time, most of us would feel awkward about inviting them both, though there are times when that could be done. Because of uncertainty as to how to handle the situation, many divorcees find them being ignored by their still married friends.

Another reason divorcees are shut out or ignored by their former friends is that in some instances, the divorce of warm friends calls attention to insecurities and tensions between those who are still married. Because of these tensions, a divorcee may be consciously or unconsciously regarded as a threat to the marriage, and so the couple may avoid their former friends for that reason. Such a couple may need to take a good look at their own marriage and establish it on a firmer foundation. Then they would do well to learn to trust each other by letting their divorced friends back in their lives. In fact, very often a newly divorced person is less a threat to someone else's marriage than anyone else in society. For a time the newly divorced has had it with marriage.

While some tact, patience, and creative imagination may be required, some contact between divorcees and former friends is sorely needed. The friends of the divorced couple could create social situations where first one and then the other of the divorced couple is included in their social functions. Social functions that do not by their nature require couples is a good example of a way to involve the divorced friend or friends. An invitation to lunch to the divorced wife by the married wife or to the divorced husband by the married husband are examples also. Here a warning may be needed however. Be wary of spending too much time talking about the former marriage. There is danger in some instances that the bitterness and the related problems of the divorcee could generate or contribute to problems between the married persons. The divorcees may need to talk about their problems. Let them, but be wary of making comparisons. I have known a couple of instances where extensive conversations between married persons and divorcees fed the dissatisfaction of the married persons and contributed to other divorces which were later regretted. All divorcees need to make new friends, but they also need the continued support of old friends. You can befriend divorcees without either prying or destroying your own marriage. Do not let them down by rejecting them.

A second suggestion I would make is that you do not make their decisions for them. Many people who have no training in counseling are tempted to tell the divorcee what to do. The concern may be legitimate, but the advice may be bad. Even if the advice is good, however, the divorced persons may take it because they did not know what to do. If the decision turns out badly, the adviser may be blamed. If you would help, encourage divorcees to consider their alternatives, clarify their own minds, and make their own decisions. Let them know that you are available if they need a friend.

I recently counseled with a couple whose marriage I tried in vain to help them save, but in the process I never tried to make decisions for either of them. On the contrary, I assured them repeatedly that, whether we could save their marriage, I wanted to continue my friendship with both. They believed me and the mutual warm friendship with each of them is even stronger now than before their divorce. We suffered together in the trauma of the decision-making process, and we are still suffering together in the process of divorce adjustment in each case. It was not easy for me to maintain the kind of attitude that made continued friendship possible, but I believe it was necessary. In any case it expressed the genuine personal commitment I felt for each of them. True friendship is tested by our willingness to allow our friends to sometimes make decisions that we wish they had not made and still befriend them.

Finally, and closely related, do not treat and do not allow others with whom you have influence to treat divorcees as second-class citizens. Many divorcees have the feeling that others regard them as second-class citizens. While in some cases this may be a kind of temporary paranoia, in other cases it is a correct perception of reality. Unfortunately, this problem is particularly notable in the church, for here we still have a few Pharisees around. Do not become a self-righteous Pharisee before your divorced friends. Some of the finest people you and I know have been divorced; for reasons I have tried to make clear, you have no right to be condescending to them. They need your love, understanding, and continued acceptance more now than ever. Give it to them.

Notes

1. R. Lofton Hudson, *Til Divorce Do Us Part* (New York: Thomas Nelson Inc., 1973), pp. 13 *ff*.

2. Mary Ann Singleton, *Life After Marriage: Divorce As a New Beginning* (New York: Stein and Day, 1974), p. 32 *ff*.

3. Ashley Mantagu, *The Meaning of Love* (New York: The Julian Press, 1953), p. 4.

4. James J. Lynch, *The Broken Heart: The Medical Consequences of Loneliness* (New York: Basic Books, 1977), p. 215.

5. Ibid., ch. 8.

6. Dietrich Bonhoeffer, *Life Together* (London: SCM Press, 1949), Chapters 2, 3.

7. Ira J. Tanner, *Loneliness: The Fear of Love* (New York: Harper and Row, 1973), p. 14.

8. Edmond Addeo and Robert Burger, *Inside Divorce: Is It What You Really Want?* (Radnor, Pa.: Chilton Books, 1975), pp. 296 *ff.*

9. Edmund Bergler, *Divorce Won't Help* (New York: Harper and Row, 1948), pp. 1-21.

10. Mel Krantzler, *Creative Divorce: An Opportunity for Personal Growth* (New York: Lippencott, 1973), p. 109 *ff.*

11. Ibid.

12. George Levinger and Oliver C. Moles, eds., *Divorce and Separation: Conditions, Causes and Consequences* (New York: Basic Books, 1979), p. 202 *ff.*

13. *Florida Times Union*, June 30, 1976.

6

Hazards and Advantages of Living Alone

Some divorcees have been so hurt by marriage that they declare they will never marry again. Others definitely intend to remarry. One of the realities with which every divorcee has to reckon is the loneliness that has to be endured. One woman confided in me that she had no intention of remarrying, but she found the loneliness almost unbearable. Some divorcees have no problem dealing with loneliness, but many do. This chapter is dedicated especially to those who do not wish to be alone, but, for a variety of reasons, find it necessary to do so. Whether you remarry or not, most of you who are divorced will have to deal with the problem of loneliness. Being alone and being lonely are not necessarily the same thing. The point I wish to make in this chapter is that, if you develop some understanding of loneliness and learn to handle it creatively, it can be a blessing rather than a curse. To the practical suggestions I made in chapter 4 I wish to add some theoretical understanding which should make the practical implementation of these suggestions easier.

The Urgency of Dealing with Loneliness

It is important to understand and respond creatively to the fact of living alone for several reasons. The first reason is that the potential dangers of loneliness are very great. The second reason is that the problem of loneliness is a universal problem. This may not seem so because some people handle the problem more creatively than others. Those who complain of loneliness have not learned to deal with the problem in constructive ways. A third reason for dealing creatively with living alone is simply that the number of persons living alone is increasing. The number of singles, including widows, never marrieds, and divorcees, has been increasing steadily in our society for several years. Despite the fact that most divorcees remarry, the number of divorcees who live alone is increasing, and even those who remarry have to face the potential problem of loneliness in the time period between marriages. It is important to do so because, despite the expectation, remarriage does not always dispel the problem of loneliness. On the contrary, sometimes it accentuates it because one's mate may not understand it.

Causes of Loneliness

Although some people experience loneliness, they do not appear to be lonely because they deal with loneliness creatively. I have a single friend in his forties who has never married who fits this category very well. He knows the pain of loneliness, but it is not a deadly pain to him because his life-style illustrates some of the suggestions for dealing with the problem. Why do others have such difficulty in dealing with the fact of being alone? Why does being alone become such an acutely and continuing painful experience for some? What causes the feeling of loneliness? While there seems to be no simple answer that can be related precisely to every example of loneliness, several causes seem worthy of consideration. I am indebted to several writers and a number of friends for these answers.

First, loneliness may be due in part to the kind of culture in which we live. In a sense this may be the reason that loneliness is a universal problem. This point was made many years ago by Thomas Wolfe.[1] Wolfe wrote that four factors in our culture contribute to the problem of loneliness. The first is the orientation to group culture which easily stifles individuality and leaves the individual with the empty feeling of being alone even in a crowd. This aspect of our cultural problem was eloquently explained and documented in the 1950s by David Riesman's book *The Lonely Crowd*.[2] What has happened since then, despite the emphasis on the self-development and individualism of the seventies, is that the crowd has become larger. A second factor in our culture which contributes to the problem of loneliness, according to Wolfe, is the size of our country. The sense of being alone is accentuated by it. A third factor Wolfe cites is the crowding of cities. Since Wolfe wrote, many sections of our country have shifted from being predominantly rural to becoming predominantly urban. Thus, the problem of crowding is more acute now that it was. Several studies have suggested, moreover, that crowding is psychologically unhealthy in other ways. Finally, Wolfe says that the competitive activism and the drive for success causes many who cannot or are not inclined to compete successfully to feel out of place and lonely. Being a divorcee may simply accentuate a problem that is common to everyone in our society.

A second cause of loneliness is noted by Jean and Veryl Rosenbaum in commenting on the Wolfe essay just mentioned. They say that the lonely person is likely to have a poor self-image.[3] The factors cited by Wolfe could easily contribute to such.

A third cause of loneliness, the fear of loving, is stressed by Ira Tanner.[4] Tanner agrees with Wolfe that loneliness is a universal problem. He says we are lonely because we are afraid to love.[5] He says that our fear of loving is affected primarily by our fundamental attitude to others. Basing his argument on his analysis of the four life views described by transactional analysis, Tanner also shows that loneliness is one's own self-evaluation. Though he does not quote the New Testament, he stresses the responsibility of the individual the same way the New Testament writers do. His basic argument is in line with John who wrote, "There is no fear in love; but perfect love casteth out fear" (1 John 4:18). Tanner's argument that many are lonely because they have found love painful and are afraid to love again has merit. One of the most painful examples of loneliness I have seen was a mother who, because of his misconduct, ordered her son out of the house and told him she never wanted to see him again. She may not, but she will probably live with the pain of loneliness for the rest of her life. She explained how she had loved him and concluded: "And look at the kind of gratitude I get." She was afraid to love him anymore. Tanner says that love involves risk, and we are reluctant to love because of the risk. But we increase our loneliness when we are unwilling to run the risk.[6]

A fourth cause of loneliness is job dissatisfaction. William Reich wrote in *The Greening of America* that millions of Americans hate their work.[7] If his perception is accurate, the reasons are not clear. A central factor may be that some professions or occupations are given greater status than others in our society. Another factor may be that many people seem forced by circumstances into jobs that are not challenging to them and are boring. Jean and Veryl Rosenbaum suggest that if your job makes you lonely you should change it. In some cases that would be an easy suggestion to implement. In other instances it would be easier said than done. This problem may sometimes be easier solved for the divorcee than others. Multitudes of divorcees find themselves locked into jobs and circumstances that seem to intensify their loneliness but from which they are not able to extricate themselves. One friend who did not want a divorce, but was abandoned by her husband, took the opportunity to go back to school and prepare for the type of job she had wanted for a long time. Today she has a job that is very satisfying and manages her problem of loneliness with much greater ease.

A fifth cause of loneliness, according to the Rosenbaums,[8] is the habit of avoiding problems that need solving but that do not go away. The habit of evading a problem needing attention may result from habits unwittingly inflicted on us as children. An example is offering a child a cookie to get his mind off a problem. In adulthood such a habit self-induced may lead to obesity or alcoholism or, I would add, to addiction to tobacco. These are unsatisfactory escape routes and end in intensifying the problem of loneliness when it returns.

A sixth cause of loneliness mentioned also by the Rosenbaums is the feeling of being unloved.[9] Here is the root of the problem of the fear of loving which is stressed by Tanner. Both Tanner and the Rosenbaums suggest that the beginning of this problem is in early childhood. There is some evidence that the feeling of being unwanted or unloved beginning in early childhood contributes to the feeling of loneliness that may continue throughout life.

A friend of mine, now divorced, said she had been lonely all her life. When I asked about her childhood, she reported that as a child she felt unwanted and unloved and that her mother often introduced her or referred to her to others as her "mistake." The mother (now deceased) probably never knew what lasting pain and loneliness would result. Since I have known her mother, I am confident she did not intend to hurt her child. The pain of loneliness is still there, though the daughter is now slowly learning to deal with it more constructively than in the past. The answer to this problem is, of course, found in the good news of the gospel of Jesus Christ which rings out the eternal message: "You are loved and wanted." God, your heavenly parent, loves you with an everlasting and perfect love, with which no human love can compare.

A final cause of loneliness is the choices the individual makes. Here an important point made by Tanner needs to be considered and developed further. He says that our loneliness is mostly our own responsibility but that we tend to blame it on others. What we need to recognize is that some of our choices, whether right or wrong, may create a distance between us and others and contribute to our feeling of aloneness. The point is that, while many of the causes which have been described may contribute to our feeling of loneliness, they do so because of the way we decide to respond to them. This fact is fundamental to the understanding of the other causes.

Understanding some of the causes of loneliness helps; but if loneliness is a universal problem, then an understanding of the complex causes is important. There is no *one* cause of loneliness. There are rather many causes. Similarly, it seems to me that there are many kinds of loneliness. Some of these will be discussed in the paragraphs that follow. The point about choices is also fundamental to the understanding of the different kinds of loneliness we may experience. An analysis of some of the forms of loneliness we may experience may help us to understand ourselves and others and may help us in the process of making the kind of responsible choices which will reduce the pain of loneliness. The analysis may also help us to make more constructive uses of the experience of being alone.

Different Kinds of Loneliness

One kind of loneliness is the kind that often accompanies divorce or death. It comes to both marriage partners and the children of divorce. To feel the pain of loneliness when one loses a loved one through death or divorce is human. The feeling is, therefore, a healthy sign for a time. Choosing to respond to this feeling in a healthy and constructive way can lead to healing.

A second kind of loneliness is the loneliness of apathy and indifference. This kind of loneliness may take either of two forms. First, it may take the form of an inner response to one's plight and to the response of others in which one concludes that nobody cares. David experienced this kind of loneliness when he said "refuge failed me; no man cared for my soul" (Ps.

142:4). This form of loneliness too is human. A second form of the loneliness of apathy and indifference is the choice of that attitude in response to the feeling that others do not care. This form is expressed in the decision that I will not care either. The tragedy is that this response only increases the sense of loneliness one feels.

A third kind of loneliness is the loneliness of being misunderstood. Many children feel misunderstood. Many husbands and wives both during and following the breakup of the marriage do not understand each other and do not feel that they are understood. This, too, is a human and probably, as Jean Paul Sartre suggests in his play *No Exit,* a universal problem. All of us are misunderstood sometimes and the feeling of not being understood is a very lonely feeling indeed. Conflicts in ideology and religious differences can easily contribute to this kind of loneliness. Working hard at dialogue can sometimes bring about a miracle whereby this kind of loneliness can be overcome.[10]

A fourth kind of loneliness is the loneliness of the suicide or the person who considers suicide. The suicidal person, of course, represents a combination of causes and forms, including especially the feelings that no one cares and that no one understands. For the suicidal person, these and other factors combine to create the loneliness of being without hope. The suicidal person sees others who have much to live for, but finds no personal reason to go on living. Thus the loneliness of ultimate despair may become an overwhelming experience. Such a person has to be persuaded that there is a reason for living. Often divorcees experience this kind of loneliness.

A fifth kind of loneliness is the loneliness of personal tragedy. Most of us can take personal tragedy easier if we have the support of those on whose care we know we can depend. However, when tragedy comes and there is no one on which to lean, the loneliness can become unbearable. The author of Ecclesiastes, perhaps drawing from his own painful experiences, showed great sensitivity to this kind of loneliness. He wrote: "Two are better than one; because they have a good reward for their labour. For if they fall, the one will lift up his fellow: but woe to him that is alone when he falleth; for he hath not another to help him up" (4:9-10). Few people in society know this kind of loneliness better than the divorcee, for the breakup of the marriage is often viewed as a personal tragedy by the husband, the wife, the children, the families of both the husband and the wife, and many friends. If those friends and close relatives withdraw because they do not know how to respond to the tragedy, the sense of loneliness which results may be as great as the tragedy itself.

A sixth kind of loneliness is the loneliness of moral isolation. A tragic example in the Bible is the story in John 8:3-11 of the woman taken in the act of adultery and brought to Jesus to see what disposition he would make of her violation of moral propriety. It is noteworthy her male partner was not also brought to Jesus. This may well have heightened her sense of moral isolation and its resulting loneliness. Her own immoral act, perhaps an attempt to overcome the loneliness she felt, instead only increased it. When she was caught, the rejection by her self-righteous accusers only increased her sense of moral isolation and loneliness. People who violate the moral laws of God, of society, and their own moral selfhood create a kind of moral isolation from their fellow human beings. They often experience a terrifying kind of loneliness. Divorcees who have contributed to the breakup of the marriage by their own infidelity know the loneliness of moral isolation and guilt. They need both the kind of forgiveness and acceptance that Jesus gave to the woman taken in adultery to overcome the loneliness of moral isolation.

A seventh kind of loneliness is closely related to the preceding one, yet it is distinctively different. I refer to the loneliness of isolation and estrangement. It differs from the preceding one in the cause of the feeling of isolation and estrangement. There is a special kind of isolation and estrangement that results from one's concern for a proper relation to God. There is a special kind of loneliness that one experiences as the feeling of being abandoned by either God or one's fellow human beings. The former may be represented by Jesus' cry of anguish on the cross when he said, "My God, my God, why hast thou forsaken me?" (Matt. 27:46). The latter may be represented by Jesus' awareness of the coming crisis that his death would incur among his disciples. Sensing that despite all his efforts to prepare them they would abandon him, he warned them, perhaps pleading with them to break his prediction. He said in John 16:32, "The hour cometh, that you . . . shall leave me alone." To be alone when one feels the need of company is to be lonely indeed.

An eighth kind of loneliness is the loneliness of crowds. Jesus very likely felt this kind of loneliness, as most of us do when we are in a crowd with which we are out of step. It is striking that on several occasions at the height of his popularity and apparent success during the great Galilean ministry, Jesus left the crowds and went to be alone. It seems probable that Jesus experienced the greatest loneliness not when he was alone but when he was with a great crowd who loved the loaves and the miracles but somehow failed to understand his message. John 6 gives a classic example of this kind of loneliness. As he clarified the meaning of what Jesus said, they superimposed a wooden literalism on his meaning which totally distorted it, and they then left him. Even some of his own disciples were among the defectors. Here was a creative way of dealing with his loneliness. He faced it and asked the twelve if they would leave also. When Simon said that the disciples would stay with Jesus, his loneliness was overcome.

The answer to the problem of loneliness in the crowd is to find someone to whom you can relate who will respect, accept, and affirm your own self-identity, regardless of whether it squares with his in every detail. We cannot take their affirmation to mean the apostles understood Jesus in every detail. Sometimes the experience of loneliness in the crowd may be the only way to protect one's self-identity. To a divorcee this can be very important because the divorcee will occasionally feel the peer pressure of a new crowd or a new small group that poses a threat to the preservation of self-identity or to the development of a new identity that is authentic. Another way of responding to the crowd is by saying, "I will accept my loneliness as the price of refusing to be poured into your mold. I will be true to my self and to my calling, even if the crowd rejects me."

A ninth kind of loneliness is the loneliness of solitude and meditation. Sometimes the loneliness of being in a crowd must be faced and response must be made at that moment. There may be times, however, when that is impossible. There may be times when we need to leave the crowd in order to keep our bearings. This kind of loneliness may be deliberately chosen. While we may debate whether this loneliness by choice is really loneliness, I maintain that it is. Whether it is sick or healthy is a more fundamental question. When being alone is a choice that is made to evade responsibility and necessary choices, it may be a sick response. When one chooses to be alone in order to meditate, pray, to find oneself, or to make a decision, it can be a creative and healthy response. Even so, the feeling of loneliness may be there as one decides, *Now I must make some decisions of my own for which I alone can accept responsibility. In the making of these decisions, moreover, I must be free from the pressures of others who would make my decisions for me.* This is healthy and is, indeed, the kind of loneliness the divorcee must often choose. Jesus often chose to be alone to meditate and pray (Matt. 14:22-27). But it was only a temporary choice, for he was never completely isolated. After a time of being alone, he returned to his disciples. To return to the task of creating community is a sign of emotional and psychological health. Happy will be the divorcee who has it or finds it.

A final type of loneliness closely related to the previous type is the loneliness of leadership. Jeremiah the prophet gives classic expression to this type of loneliness when he said: "I sat alone because of thy hand" (Jer. 15:17). He was rejected and condemned by most of the religious leaders of his time. He, therefore, felt lonely and gave clear expression to his complaint. He complained both to God and to his fellow human beings. One who examines the story of Jeremiah will know that, in response to his complaint, a minority of influential friends helped him to live with the loneliness of leadership.

Similarly, Jesus knew the loneliness of leadership which resulted from the choices he made. In John 6, we are told that when Jesus perceived that the crowd was about to take him by force and make him king he withdrew. There in the wilderness again, he experienced the loneliness of knowing that his message had not been understood. As we have said, however, he maintained his self-understanding as a leader even when his closest associates considered abandoning him. He seems to have known, more-over, that this experience was a sample of what would come later. In John 16:32 he told his disciples that the time would come when they would leave him but he would not be quite alone, for the Father would still be with him. However, in the hours of agony on the cross, his loneliness as a leader may have been the greatest, as he wondered if even God had forsaken him. He cried out: "My God, my God, why hast thou forsaken me?" (Matt. 27:46).

One of his followers had betrayed him, another had denied him, and the others had scattered to return only near the end. I am confident that Jesus understands loneliness better than anyone.

One of the greatest blows that can come to a conscientious minister is the breakup of his family by divorce. Sometimes a minister who gets a divorce will be abandoned by his family and his church and will find himself unable to continue his leadership role in the church. Such a person experiences a very intense kind of loneliness. In fact, almost any leader who gets a divorce may experience the loneliness of leadership more acutely than some others because he (or she) is often cast into the position of being a role model with which others may identify. Unfortunately such a person may have become an idol both to himself and to others. Despite the loneliness one may feel, one should take some comfort in the shattering of an idol. It would be better shattered some other way, but people need to respect the humanity of their leaders, including their religious leaders. While Paul recognized that people do regard religious leaders as role models with whom to identify, he saw the danger of such a practice. Thus, he wrote: "We do not preach ourselves, but Christ Jesus" (2 Cor. 4:5, NASB). By this statement he meant that we are not to judge the faith by our model and not to model our lives according to everything we see in our models but according to what we see in Jesus Christ. The fact remains that, despite all admonitions, a leader who is divorced is exposed publicly more than others and is sometimes made to feel the pain of loneliness more acutely on that account.

The loneliness of leadership must sometimes be chosen by a leader. Paul wrote to the Thessalonians, "We thought it best to be left behind at Athens alone" (1 Thess. 3:1, NASB). He may have done this because he wanted to reflect on the next stage of development in his role as a leader after the crises he had experienced in his ministry in this area. Similarly, the leader who is in the process of divorce and/or following divorce may experience a special kind of loneliness as the question of how the divorce will affect the continuation of his role as a leader. It may or may not require a new kind of leadership; but if the divorcee responds creatively to this crisis of lonely decision making as a leader, he or she may emerge as a better leader.

Summary of the Advantages of Living Alone

Despite the hazards, living alone, like being divorced, can be a tragic experience or it can be a door of opportunity which can result in new growth. In this concluding section, I wish to call attention to some of the positive values of living alone.

First, living alone may provide the divorcee the time needed to sort out some of the causative factors in the divorce as the process of healing from the emotional injury takes place. If one focuses on learning from the experience rather than trying to fix the blame, this time can be used creatively. It takes time for emotions to cool before one can reflect calmly and with reasonable objectivity on what has happened. It may be helpful to spend some time using your imagination to try to put yourself in the place of the former marriage partner, not necessarily to seek reconciliation. But that may be neither possible nor desirable. Trying to see the problem through the eyes of the other person, however, may open the door to the letting go of hostility and the extending of forgiveness. It also may open the door to the next advantage of living alone.

Living alone may also provide the divorcee with the possibility of achieving new self-knowledge, free from external pressures. New time alone may make it possible to free oneself from the self-image that was determined by role playing. Many divorcees find that in marriage individuality has been lost or submerged, and in single life it can be recovered. This recovery is important for self-esteem regardless of whether remarriage is in the future. Several of my friends who were divorced and have remarried have told me that their first marriages ended in divorce mainly because they simply were not ready for marriage. Their second marriages are solid. In dialogue with them, it seems clear that in the time they spent living alone they discovered or decided on a concept of self that now seems authentic both to them and to me. Another way of putting it is that they were not mature when they married the first time. During the experience of divorce and living alone, they grew toward maturity as they came to know themselves. As they came to know themselves and accept themselves better, they became better prospects for a future successful marriage.

Both of these first two advantages call attention to the need for some time alone after divorce. One of the temptations that can be disastrous is the temptation to respond to the painful loneliness that follows divorce by remarrying in haste.

A third advantage of living alone is that it may provide an opportunity to achieve a healthy balance between aloneness and relatedness. One who had not learned to handle aloneness will often have problems handling relatedness. A former husband of a famous movie actress recently wrote that he discovered that his wife could not bear being alone. Apparently, since she has been married seven times, she also has difficulty relating to a husband. Dietrich Bonhoeffer has made a lasting contribution to my understanding of this problem.[11] While living alone, one can choose and control the amount and kind of relatedness that is preferred. It can be a time for learning how to relate to others in new, more creative and mature ways.

A fourth advantage of living alone is that it may provide an opportunity to go places that were impossible in marriage. Despite the danger of becoming self-centered, the freedom of movement one who lives alone may have is to many an enjoyable experience. Moreover, it may enhance the process of developing new relationships. A divorcee may often want to stay at home and go nowhere for a time. Do not feel guilty about it, but this attitude should not be allowed to linger.

A fifth advantage of living alone is closely related to the preceding one. It is that those who live alone often find that they can exercise control over their time much easier than those who live with others. The creative and responsible management of time is a duty we owe to God, to others, and to ourselves. To some divorcees this problem may not be real. To others, however, the management of time in marriage was determined either by others or by the variety of demands inherent in the necessities of family life. Many people never learn to use time wisely. Living alone can be a good time to review your use of time. Learning to use it in ways that are satisfying to you because they bring about a sense of accomplishment and enjoyment cannot only enhance your self-image but can also enhance the process of learning how to relate to others. Also, time well managed, and thus used creatively, may reduce or remove the feeling of loneliness. Further, when you learn to manage time well, you may find it easier to do those things for which you once thought you could never find the time. A good book to help with the process of using time creatively is *Managing Your Time* by Ted W. Engstrom and R. Alex MacKenzie.[12]

A final advantage of living alone is that it may, in many instances, provide an opportunity to use outside resources for self-development and growth. I encouraged one couple I counseled, who have now been divorced for several months, to take courses at a local community college. The cost is inexpensive and the contribution it is making to their growth is very great. It is helping both of them in the process of adjustment.

Notes

1. Thomas Wolfe, "The Anatomy of Loneliness," *American Mercury,* October, 1941.

2. David Riesman, *The Lonely Crowd* (Garden City, New York: Doubleday Anchor Books, 1950).

3. Jean Rosenbaum and Veryl Rosenbaum, *Conquering Loneliness* (New York: Hawthorn Books, Inc., 1973), p. 30.

4. Ira Tanner, *Loneliness: The Fear of Love* (New York: Harper and Row, 1973).

5. Ibid. p. x.

6. Ibid., p. 14.

7. William Reich, *The Greening of America* (New York: Random House, 1970), pp. 5-6.

8. Ibid., pp. 81 *ff.*

9. Ibid., chapter 7.

10. Reuel Howe, *The Miracle of Dialogue* (Greenwich, CT: Seabury Press, 1963).

11. Dietrich Bonhoeffer, *Life Together* (London: SCM Press, 1949).

12. Ted W. Engstrom and R. Alex MacKenzie, *Managing Your Time* (Grand Rapids: Zondervan, 1968).

7
Whether to Remarry:
The Hazards and Possibilities

Whether to remarry is a question which appears to trouble many divorcees who are serious-minded Christians who are also deeply involved in the life of the church. The fundamental question for many of them is whether remarriage would mean they were living in adultery. Others simply wonder if they could make another marriage work. Still others, finding the pain of loneliness severe, remarry at the first opportunity only to find themselves in another miserable situation. The purpose of this chapter is to encourage the divorcee to consider some of the hazards and possibilities of remarriage so that if and when the divorcee does remarry the possibilities of success in the marriage can be enhanced.

In an earlier chapter I have interpreted the biblical teaching as not providing an absolute prohibition of divorce and remarriage, but only those who find these explanations or similar explanations satisfactory to their own minds can apply them freely to their own situations. On the basis of my own interpretation of biblical teaching and on the basis of my own experience as a counselor, it is my judgment that some divorcees should remarry and some should not. Each has to decide in the light of one's own experience and one's situation. No one else can make that decision. However, there are some things that might be worth considering before making a decision.

Considering the Hazards of Remarriage

For one thing, the divorcee would do well to consider the hazards that might be involved in the decision to remarry. First, there is the danger that unresolved problems may spoil the new marriage. It is quite normal, as we have said, for the newly divorced to be preoccupied for some time with their own problems. One of the dangers of remarrying during the early months after the divorce is that one will enter a new marriage so preoccupied with one's own problems and needs that it is very difficult to be concerned about the needs of the other person. At the same time the other person may have the same problem. Drawn to each other because of a sharing of pain and the extending of sympathy may seem for a time to create a natural bond. However, the underlying emotions may suddenly bring out a strange response if one had enough self-insight to recognize it. The response may be, "Listen, I cannot help you with your problems. I have too many of my own. I married you to get help for myself."

Another response may come from one partner who has resolved his or her problems and now feels free. The response here may be one of disappointment and even rage that the other partner still has emotional hang-ups that make a free and enthusiastic response impossible. Either of these persons may reason, *I thought I would be better off if I remarried, but I am not. I might as well call it quits.* Before considering remarriage, therefore, you should consider carefully whether you have gone through the aftermath of divorce and whether the healing process is sufficiently advanced to make unselfish, self-giving love possible again.

A second hazard of remarrying concerns the effect remarriage may have on any children involved. The children may not accept the new spouse at first; and in some cases, depending on their age and other factors, they may never accept the new spouse at all. Both of these possibilities need to be taken into consideration by those who are considering remarriage.

For a successful remarriage involving children, both partners in the new relationship must recognize several factors which may affect the happiness of the marriage. First, the couple needs to accept the children unconditionally. That is, the love given to the children must not be made dependent on a loving response. Both partners need to give the children time to accept the new partner. Second, both partners must determine not to let the acceptance or the nonacceptance of the new parent by the children affect their own personal relationship to each other. At first the bestowal of love on a new parent may be viewed by the children as a betrayal of their own relationship with the other parent. But in the long run, the emotional health of the children will be fostered by the creation of a loving relationship between the marriage partners. Third, both partners need to accept the need of the children to have a continuing relationship with the absent parent. Sometimes this need is very difficult to meet, especially where the remaining parent and the children have been mistreated by the absent parent. If the new marriage is to be most successful, however, this acceptance is often necessary both for the parent's own happiness and for the happiness of the husband-wife relationship.

In fact a recent study by W. Glenn Clingempeel, a psychologist at Temple University, suggests that those remarried divorcees who see their ex-spouses on a regular basis (usually in connection with the children) were on the whole happier than those who saw them rarely. They were also happier than those who saw them very often. Specifically he said that those who saw their former spouses around once a month were happier than either those who saw them every week or those who saw them only three or four times a year. The prime factor here is very likely the effect on the children, and it occurs to me that the effect the contact with the former spouse may vary according to the situation.[1]

A third hazard that must often be faced in the consideration of remarriage is that the new mate may not accept any continued relationship with the former mate that may sometimes be necessary. For example, in dealing with alimony payments, property settlements, and a variety of similar matters, the new marriage partner may occasionally need to have contact by phone, letter, or personal contact with the former mate. If the remarriage is not securely grounded in mutual trust, these contacts can be threatening to the new relationship. Therefore, in considering remarriage, it would be wise to discuss this projected problem quite frankly with one's future mate. A similar example would be where there are children involved. Sometimes, one who remarries suddenly discovers that the new mate resents any kind of contact with the former spouse. When there are children involved, visitation rights often make some contacts absolutely necessary. Remarriage where there are children involved can be very complicated, and every individual who considers remarriage would do well to consider some of the complications.

A fourth hazard those who are considering remarriage should consider is the economic problems that may be involved, including problems related to alimony, child support, and family support as a whole. The breakup of a marriage can be expensive. So can the contraction of a new marriage, especially when one of the marriage partners has to continue alimony and/ or child support from a former marriage for some years after a new marriage has been solemnized. The division of income between alimony and child support for the previous marriage and support for the new marriage can create severe economic anxiety. Disagreements over financial matters can make the strains of a second marriage even more intense than they were in the first marriage. Those who consider remarriage, therefore, should take a very careful look at the economic prospects, planning a budget which takes as much as possible into account. The couple considering remarriage should also be sure they are in agreement on the acceptance of whatever financial limitations that will be necessary for them to live together.

A fifth hazard for the remarriage of a divorcee is the temptation to make comparisons with the former spouse. This temptation is a particularly great hazard when disagreements develop and one partner makes comparisons which put the new partner in a bad light. Several rules for good communication may prevent some serious difficulties. First, when criticism is necessary and one is tempted to make comparisons, let the comparisons be between what is and what ought to be rather than between the present and the past mate. Second, let the criticism be constructive with emphasis on positive suggestions. Third, when one is tempted to make comparisons with the former mate, let the stress be on positive comparisons where the present mate is put in a good light. Accentuate the positive. Sometimes it may be necessary for the couple to agree not to talk about their former spouses. Often, however, the divorcee has a need to get some feelings about a former mate out in the open and needs the patience and understanding of the other partner in order to do so. There may be cases where the agreement not to talk about the former spouse may be a mistake.

Some of the healthiest and happiest remarriages I have seen have been between people who felt completely free to speak of their former mates in the presence of their present marital partner. Indeed, this freedom and mutual acceptance of each other as formerly married may be an important test of the success of the new marriage. In some instances this freedom can be achieved before the second marriage. Conversation about the previous mate, however, is less likely to be a threat to the new marriage if freedom to talk about one's previous mate is achieved before the new marriage. This likelihood suggests, therefore, that one should not rush into a new marriage until the emotions that were associated with the breakup of the previous marriage have calmed down considerably.

Generally, it is better to avoid comparisons with others and accept one's new partner with all the uniqueness that God gives to each of us. The depths and riches of each individual person are to be discovered, cultivated, and developed. The new marriage can most likely be successful if, among other things, each partner can feel free to talk about the former mate, but does not feel constrained either to do so or to encourage or discourage the other partner from doing so.

A final hazard to be observed in considering remarrying is the temptation either to expect too little or too much in the new marriage. The temptation to expect too little in the new marriage may reflect the kind of cynicism and bitterness which indicates unresolved problems from the previous marriage which can easily threaten the health and stability of the new marriage. Moreover, the temptation to expect too little may often result in the tendency to give too little to make the new marriage work. Marriage is a matter of mutual self-giving, and those who do not think they have to give much are courting disaster for the marriage.

The opposite temptation, the temptation to enter a new marriage expecting too much, is equally hazardous. This temptation may cause the failure of a first marriage when there are really not many other problems. Some people enter marriage thinking it will solve all their problems only to find that it adds new ones. You may have heard that marriages are made in heaven. Perhaps so, but they are consummated and lived out on earth. Sometimes a marriage partner will spoil the possibilities of success for the marriage by expecting too much either of oneself or of one's partner. Marriage is in some ways a bed of roses, but anyone who grows roses will tell you that roses have thorns. If you love roses, you have to accept the thorns that go with them. The person who says, "My first marriage was a mess, but my next one will be perfect," may be too naive. It is a noble thing to determine not to repeat the mistakes of the first marriage; but for any marriage to succeed, both partners must learn that it involves both mutual love and forgiveness, which requires the willingness to accept each other, faults and all, and to survive the differences and the problems as well as the joys that go with it. What Dietrich Bonhoeffer said of the church is often true of marriage: one who judges his own church (marriage) by his own ideal picture of the church (marriage) will begin by hating the church (marriage) and will end by hating himself most of all. The church (marriage) is to be accepted as God's gift, to be cultivated and cherished, not condemned.[2] It is the reality within which Christians live. Similarly, a divorcee who remarries should be prepared to accept the new mate as God's unique gift, not to be compared either to one's former spouse or to one's own ideal picture of what a spouse should be or of what a marriage should be. In considering remarriage, the main stress for each individual should be on becoming the best person one can be and on making the marriage the best that it might be.

There are some things about each of our personality structure that are very difficult to change, and others that are impossible to change. We have to live with them, and those who live with us have to accept those things we cannot change, and we have to accept those things they cannot change. Divorcees considering remarriage will do well to take careful stock of their own personality structures and that of their prospective mates and settle the question in their own minds as to what qualities can be changed and what cannot be changed. Also they should consider whether they can live in peace and happiness with those personality qualities of the other partner which cannot be changed.

Some time ago I spent only an hour counseling with a couple considering marriage who had already set the date of the wedding. Both were divorcees. The man had been married twice and was twice divorced. The woman was divorced once. She had been married to a man who was mentally ill and had waited until her children were grown to divorce him. I had heard things about the man's personality that disturbed me. While I could neither report nor use such hearsay, I did talk to them about the importance of communication concerning both those things they had in common and their differences. I asked them if they had had a frank discussion about their expectations in marriage. While they answered yes, somehow I did not sense in their answers the ring of authenticity. A few days later the man called me and reported that they had postponed the wedding because they had agreed that they had not gotten to know each other very well. I have not seen or heard from them since. My tentative conclusion is that they discovered that each of them had conflicting expectations of marriage that their marriage would not have been able to deliver. Our counseling session may have prevented a disaster.

The Possibilities of Remarriage

In the discussion of Jesus' teaching on divorce in Matthew 19, I suggested that, according to my understanding of Jesus' teaching, some people could not and should not be married, that some could and should get married and stay married, and that some who married could not keep the marriage together. I concluded that those who could be married and keep the marriage together should do so. Here I suggest that something similar is true of divorcees. Some divorcees should not remarry. Some are like Kierkegaard who decided never to marry because of his peculiar personality problems. Those who are like Kierkegaard and marry, only to find their marriage ending in divorce despite their honest efforts to prevent it, may find it unwise to try again. That does not mean they are failures as persons, and they should not be so regarded by their friends. Most of us would be failures at some things, but that does not mean we are failures in any general sense.

Other divorcees should remarry. I know of no simple rule as to who should and who should not. In the final analysis, given the opportunity, only the individual can decide this question. However, I would like to describe some positive possibilities one who genuinely desires to remarry might consider.

First, despite my argument earlier about the applicability to all persons who live alone of Lynch's argument that loneliness kills, I acknowledged that his argument has a lot of merit because there are many who have difficulty dealing with the problem of being alone. For them being alone becomes loneliness. For such persons, marriage can be an answer to the problem of being alone. It should not be the only answer because there are other ways of dealing with the problem of loneliness. Nor should loneliness be the only reason for remarriage. Nevertheless, remarriage for many will be one way by which the threat of loneliness can be overcome. The paradoxical suggestion I make, however, is that remarriage can answer the problem of loneliness best when one has remained single long enough to live with the problem and to have learned how to appreciate the privilege of life together. It seems to me that marriage is a better answer to the problem of loneliness when the prime reason for remarriage is not to free oneself from it. Many people who are happily remarried have told me that loneliness was one factor, but not the main factor in their remarriage. The fact that some have such difficulty in dealing with the problem of loneliness means that remarriage may be for them a significant factor in the preservation of their emotional health.

A second possibility which might be taken into account by those who are considering remarriage is that the children involved may have better care. The experience of some children in foster homes provides a parallel example. I have known of cases where children in foster homes did not wish to return to their own parents even when they were forced to do so. Children need two parents, and while it is not always possible in today's society and circumstances, it is highly desirable. Sometimes when there is no healthy relationship between the children and the former spouse, remarriage may provide the best opportunity for providing an environment where the children can grow to maturity. While it is potentially dangerous to remarry solely or even primarily for the sake of the children, the possibility of helping the children is a fundamental reason. The danger is that one's new mate may feel neglected and unloved. At the same time, I have known of cases where, although concern for the children was the prime reason for remarriage, the marriage turned out to be both happy and successful. Frank discussion of the details and responsibilities involved in caring for children, however, is very important. This discussion is particularly important where one of the marriage partners has not been a parent before. It is even more important where one has been a parent but has never taken the responsibilities of parenthood seriously. Where both partners in the remarriage have a good relationship with each other, share with each other in taking their parental responsibilities seriously, and, where it is possible to do so, maintain some healthy relationships with former spouses, remarriage can contribute greatly to the emotional security of the children.

A third possibility which may be realized in remarriage is that the fulfillment of personhood can be easier. While there are many factors involved in the fulfillment of personhood and many ways of achieving that goal, for some divorcees remarriage is an important way of increasing a sense of personal fulfillment. Several divorcees have told me that they genuinely liked being married and after being married have never quite been able to think of themselves as single again. The fact that most divorcees remarry is strong evidence that most divorcees may think the same way. A number of divorcees have told me that in their first marriages they enjoyed some real happiness until some unanticipated crisis or a series of crises broke their marriages apart. Until then they really felt fulfilled as persons. Many people find new fulfillment as persons in a second marriage. Where remarriage is not possible or for various reasons not desirable, there are other healthy and respectable ways of achieving personal fulfillment. Many find personal fulfillment in a profession or service vocation.

A fourth possibility that may be realized in remarriage is that social acceptance in some circles is much easier. Today many social groups accept both divorce and remarriage more readily than has been the case in the past. Unfortunately, however, many singles between marriages find themselves ostracized from many groups which have been and still are important to them. Although the ostracism is not always deliberate, the result is just as real and painful to the divorcee as it would be if it were deliberate. Sometimes the only way to get back in some social circles is to remarry. This problem is made more acute for singles by the fact that many of the singles groups they know share a life-style that is offensive to them.

The alternative for such singles may be to create a new singles group or find a new one or remarry. One of the best places to find a new singles group whose life-style is highly moral is in the church. In the church, moreover, a single is more likely to find social acceptance in many different groups than almost anywhere else. Even here sometimes, however, it is difficult, though it should not be. The church also is a good place to find both a prospective mate and social acceptance in a variety of groups. Even here, it is easier to find acceptance with a wide variety of organizations within the church if one is married. Until recently, most of the organizations of the church have been family oriented. On balance, while there are many new organizations for singles in church and society, there are advantages in being married, for it is still the case that some circles are entered more easily by the married.

A fifth possibility that may be important to some divorcees is to prove that one is not a failure as a person and as a marriage partner. Many divorcees continue to have the haunting feeling that, since they have failed in one of life's most important ventures, they are failures. Their feeling of failure in that experience may damage their self-confidence in general and may result in the fear of failure in pursuing other important ventures. This reasoning is fallacious because some who are, in fact, failures in marriage are nevertheless very successful in other important ventures.

Many people who fail miserably in their first marriages succeed magnificently in the second try.[3] In fact some studies suggest that most second marriages last. Most likely the reason for this is that most people learn from the mistakes they made in the first marriage, and what they learn is what assures the success of the second marriage. It is important for some who are open to self-understanding and to learning from their mistakes to prove themselves with a second marriage. Some individuals need the boost in their sense of self-worth that comes from success in this important venture. There is danger, however, that one who has serious doubts about the possibility of success in a second marriage can reduce the possibility of success by uncertainty. Therefore, in order to prove yourself, you have to develop both self-knowledge and self-confidence.

A final possibility that may be realized in remarriage is that one can share with others what one has learned, first in the experience of marriage failure and second in the experience of the success in the new marriage. Not everyone has the self-insight that is necessary for objective sharing, and some may lack the communication skills to share what they have learned. Many, however, can be very helpful to others because of their experience. It is widely assumed in the organization of classes on divorce adjustment that divorcees can learn for each other and can learn together from trained counselors. What is often overlooked is the possibility that many divorcees could be of great help to three other groups of persons, especially those divorcees who are succeeding in second marriages. First, they could be of help to those whose marriages are in trouble and are considering divorce. Second, they could be of help to those who are considering marriage for the first time. Third, they could be of help to those who are still going through the trauma of their first divorces. Last, but not least, the divorcee who is considering remarriage knows that the only sure way to know how successful he or she has been in the process of learning from mistakes is to risk another marriage.

When to Remarry

The question often arises in the mind of a divorcee as to when to remarry. Assuming that one has decided to remarry if the opportunity comes, how soon should that be? While there is no simple answer to the question and the reply we might give in one case might not do for another, it appears that there are some general considerations which most people would do well to consider. Some might say, remarry when you have the opportunity. Such an approach could end in catastrophe. The timing is very important even when the opportunity appears to be a good one. This point is central to all the factors to be considered.

Time to Heal

First, one may feel free to remarry when the main process of healing of the emotional injuries resulting from the first marriage is over. A common error made by many divorcees is that they remarry while the wounds of the previous marriage are still fresh. It is important to give the healing process time. While it is not possible to suggest how much time is needed for each individual because it may vary widely, there are some very important factors related to the decision as to when enough time has elapsed. One is the question of whether you have decided to let the wounds heal or whether you are keeping them from healing. Basic to the process of healing is the willingness to forgive and be forgiven. Although the amount of stress and pain involved may vary according to the circumstances, the readiness to forgive and put those experiences behind you is fundamental to the hastening of the healing process.

The second factor is the willingness to let time do its work. Time is a great healer. Some may be impatient and say they do not have much time. Others may simply be impatient and want to act quickly when some things should not be rushed. In your patience you may not only possess your soul but you may also possess your next marriage. Part of the problem may be that, if you rush into a new marriage before the healing process has occurred, the continued pain may reduce the patience level, which can contribute to the spoiling of the new marriage. Learn the patience of waiting before the new marriage, and you will increase the chances of success. Numerous friends who have successful second marriages have told me that they married too soon the first time, that they were really not ready for marriage. Before they remarried they gave themselves a good bit of time, from a year to five years, before they tried again.

This point is very important but a word of caution must be added. Sometimes the wounds inflicted on the person in a broken marriage are so severe that, despite one's best efforts, the pain never quite goes away. Is remarriage to be forbidden for such a person? I would not think so, but one must recognize the continued pain and neither hide it nor allow oneself to be preoccupied with it. One's future spouse must be aware of it and accept it as a part of the reality with which the couple must live. If there has been enough time and the couple both recognize and accept the problem, the mutual sharing can make it easier than bearing the burden of pain alone. Also, it is important to recognize that, in many instances, emotional scars from the first marriage will last throughout life, and those emotional scars may always be tender. Thus, the point I have made about waiting until the healing process has occurred could be taken too seriously. Most, if not all, of us have some emotional scars which we carry throughout life. Those of us who live creatively in the intimacy of family life have to learn about each other's emotional scars and avoid inflicting damage on them.

Finally, it is often wise to let the waiting period not only include time for some healing of the wounds from the previous marriage but also time for a get-acquainted period with one's prospective new mate. When the couple planning a second marriage can talk freely about the problems and wounds they have from the previous marriage without becoming emotionally upset, and when the discussion does not affect their present relationship, they may be ready for a second marriage. It takes time to prepare for marriage. Take your time.

Time to Learn

One may be ready for remarriage when one has learned from the mistakes that contributed to the breakup of the previous marriage. These mistakes should include not only the things you might have avoided that could have contributed to the difficulty but also the responses you may have made to your partner's mistakes. Sometimes, the temptation to forget the first marriage is very strong. Although there comes a time to do that, one should first assess the process of the breakup in retrospect. When you are confident that you have learned from your mutual mistakes, you may be ready for remarriage. Some, of course, may be very uncertain about this point, for sometimes the problem is very hard to assess. For example, when the final separation comes from an argument that in retrospect really seems very minor, as is often the case, one or both persons may be confused about the real problem. There may be a need for counsel in such cases. The method is less important than the learning itself.

Time to Manage Problems

One may be ready for remarriage when one has learned to manage one's own personal problems, especially the problem of guilt which may be a carryover from the first marriage. In addition to the need for forgiveness and for learning, the divorcee needs to develop a creative way of dealing with the guilt problem. Many serious-minded Christians find difficulty with what the Bible appears to them to say about divorce and remarriage. One woman with whom I have counseled, for example, remarried but somehow could not escape the feeling that she was living in adultery. Another had to endure the suggestion from unkind friends that she was living in adultery. Oddly enough, I have not heard of anyone suggesting to male divorcees who remarried that they were living in adultery.

Using the biblical interpretation developed in an earlier chapter, I have fortunately been able to help many divorcees who remarried to become free of this feeling of guilt. However, it seems to me that it is far better to deal with this problem before remarriage. The problem of guilt may be largely a matter of changing one's understanding about what the New Testament really teaches about divorce and remarriage and how that teaching should be applied. It may also be related to the problem of time needed for healing. That is, even when one has resolved the intellectual, theological, and moral problems involved, some time may be needed to allow the emotions to adjust to the decision. It is important, however, that one's choice of a moral solution is an honest one. Otherwise serious emotional conflicts can be the result.

In addition to the problem of guilt, one can enter a new marriage with greater freedom and enthusiasm when other problems have been brought under control. These problems may include satisfaction in one's vocational choice and whether to continue the same vocation after marriage. They may include the willingness to move to another house, town, or state. They may include attitudes toward parents, children, or any other close relatives whose relationship might affect the success of the marriage.

Opportunity

A fourth factor which may affect the question of when to remarry is whether or not you have an opportunity that holds real promise of success. I cannot avoid the conclusion that many divorcees find the pain of loneliness so great that they are tempted to consider *any opportunity* which emerges. That can be tragic. On one hand, I suggest that it might be better to remain single than to rush into remarriage at the first opportunity. On the other hand, I suggest that many divorcees remarry when, after solving the numerous problems which have been mentioned, they find a prospective new partner with whom success seems possible. Marriage is always a risk of faith, and many of us could not wait until we were absolutely sure of success in advance. What we must do is size up the prospects honestly and prayerfully and give it our best.

Economic Circumstances

Finally, and closely related to the preceding point, one may be free to remarry when the economic circumstances are right. This point is as important as it is difficult to assess properly and clearly. One may debate, for example, whether the economic circumstances were right when we married, but my wife and I were agreed in facing the economic problems ahead of us together. I had four years of college and six years of graduate school ahead of me. At least we saw the possibility of economic survival, counted the cost in terms of self-sacrifice, and prepared to pay the price. Some divorcees are divorcees in part because they failed to count the economic costs. Disagreement over money is a common factor in marital difficulty. Some divorcees repeat the same error in remarriage, for second marriages can sometimes involve very complicated economic problems. Those who are considering remarriage may be ready when, with their future mates, they have worked out a budget that takes into account basic necessities, contingencies, and the financial resources to meet them.

When these factors have been considered, remarriage may be a desirable choice for a divorcee.

Notes

1. *Family Weekly,* June 27, 1982.
2. Dietrich Bonhoeffer, *Life Together* (London: SCM Press, 1949), pp. 17-18.
3. According to Glick and Norton, 38 of 100 first marriages will end in divorce, 75% of divorcees will remarry, and 44% of those who remarry will eventually divorce again. This means that 56% of second marriages will last. It also means that the divorce rate is higher among those who remarry. This fact puzzles sociologists.

It is noteworthy however, that their statistics suggest that most first marriages and second marriages last. pp. 339-340. Cited by William R. Garrett, *Seasons of Marriage and Family Life.* (New York: Holt, Rinehart and Winston, 1982), pp. 339-340. This and other studies indicate that second marriages are more likely than first marriages to end in divorce. Cf. Letha Dawson Scanzoni and John Scanzoni, *Men Women and Change: A Sociology of Marriage and Family.* (New York: McGraw Hill, 1976), p. 666.

8
Helping the Children Adjust

For many outside observers, one of the most tragic aspects of divorce is its effects on the children. While the effects may vary widely, there is wide consensus that divorce is a traumatic experience for children. The estimates of the seriousness of the damage done to the children vary from the view that children *never* get over the divorce of their parents to the view that children of divorce are on the whole happier and better adjusted than those of the general population. While it is very difficult to generalize about this matter, and especially difficult to validate accurate comparisons with the general population, there is evidence to suggest that the truth lies somewhere between the two extremes. It also seems clear to me that the problems of the children of divorce are in some ways similar to the problems of the children in unhappy marriages. Sometimes these problems become more acute when the divorce occurs, and in other cases they may become less acute. It seems certain that today more children are involved in divorce than ever before. While the nature of the connections between divorce, unhappy marriages, and some of the tragic statistics on children is not clear, it seems likely to me that there are some connections.

For example, in 1981 more than 100,000 were kidnapped by one of their own parents. There is likely to be connections between these statistics and the number of children who disappear, never to be found again. Four thousand children are murdered each year, many by their own parents. Suicides among young people have increased 75 percent since 1976 and over 300 percent since 1960. During the same period the divorce rate has tripled. As a prison minister for two years, I discovered that most of the prisoners I came to know over a two-year period, spending four hours a week interviewing and counseling, came from broken or unhappy homes. Many studies indicate also that the number of battered children has increased considerably in the last few years.

112

Anne Harris Cohn says, moreover, that most of the violence against children comes out of family frustration.[1] Despite the uncertainty of the exact connections between the alarming facts presented here and the wide variety of other factors which may play a role in producing the tragic statistics, it seems obvious that one of the most important things divorcees with children can do is to agree to do everything possible to help the children adjust to the new situation which results from the divorce.

The importance of doing the very best that can be done for the children is strongly underscored by Dr. David Goodman, marriage counselor and child psychologist.[2] Goodman says children *never* get over a divorce, that they feel rejected because they conclude that the parents did not love them enough to reconcile their differences. He says that nothing can replace what a divorce-orphaned child has lost. Similarly, while she is generally more positive about her own adjustment to the divorce of her parents, Julie List reports that even in college with her parents' divorce several years behind her, she still grieved over the loss of something most children take for granted. At the same time she said that always believing that her parents loved her was a great help.[3] She reported further that a milestone in the recovery of security was passed when several years after the divorce, her parents finally became friends. Yet, in spite of the love that continued, there was always a sense of something missing.[4] Even if this view is an extreme one, as some would be inclined to argue, it still calls attention to the importance of what divorced parents should do to help the children involved to live with the tragedy. To put it more positively, if it is possible for the children of divorcees to come through the trauma of divorce and grow up to live happy lives, then the parents owe it to themselves and to their children to do whatever they can to enhance these possibilities.

The purpose of this chapter is to call attention to a number of negative and positive suggestions which may guide divorced parents in helping their children not only adjust but also to learn things which will increase the possibility of their achieving success and happiness.

Preparing the Children

For some, the suggestion made here will come too late, but for those who are still considering divorce, it is a very important suggestion. It comes from the complaints of numerous children who have said the news of the divorce of their parents came as a complete shock. While some children see the divorce coming even before the parents do, others are taken by surprise. The probable reason is that many parents feel that it is in the best interest of the children to protect them from all talk of divorce. According to studies by California psychologists Judith S. Wallerstein and Joan B. Kelly, however, such efforts at protection often do more harm than good.[5] Similarly, Warner Troyer in *Divorced Kids*, wrote that he failed his own children on this point. Later after talking with between 300 and 400 children of divorce, he reported that almost every one of them reported that they had been given no warning that a divorce was imminent. Even when children are aware of problems, they usually would prefer to stay in an insecure marriage than to live separately from either parent. Most of the children, therefore, assume hopefully that the marriage will stay together despite the problems. The fact is that children are a part of the divorce process, and there is some evidence that they can adjust better if they are told about the possibility of divorce before it occurs. Sometimes children can be a source of insight that can help the parents. I have been amazed at the insight some children I have known have had into their parents problems. Taking the children into counsel in some cases cannot only reduce the anxiety in the children but also it can be a means by which parents come to better understand themselves and each other. Also, it can deepen the relationship of trust between the parents and the children.

Assessing the Blame for the Divorce

Numerous child psychologists and marriage counselors report that the children of divorce often, if not usually, blame themselves for the divorce. It is, therefore, extremely important for those who have failed to prepare the children for divorce before it occurred, to help the children soon afterward to understand what happened as far as possible. It seems understandable to me that many parents would fail to prepare the children for divorce because, in fact, many divorcees never prepared themselves for it. Many divorcees never plan to get a divorce. Even after it happens, they find themselves asking, Has this happened to me? or saying, I can't believe this is happening to me. When it happens, each divorcee should try to understand how and why it happened, not so much to assess or fix the blame on oneself or one's partner but in order to learn something that will enable one to grow. It is especially important to reassure the children that they are not to blame for the divorce.

The factors which influence the decision of the children to blame themselves for the divorce are not all clear because we only have what the children say, and it is uncertain whether their self-understanding gives them clear insight into their own feelings. It seems likely that children are less likely to hide their true feelings to themselves or to others than adults are, yet Troyer indicates that they often do hide their hurt feelings from their parents.[6] Even so, what they say about this problem may generally be taken as accurate statements of their real feelings. For example, they often reason that the fact that their parents stayed together until they had them must indicate that they (the children) are the cause of the divorce. While children seldom verbalize their self-condemnation quite this explicitly, much of what they say is consistent with this view. They reason also that if they had been better children it would not have happened.

One of the reasons parents may try to shield their children from the disagreements and from the impending divorce is that they honestly feel that they are protecting children from something they would have difficulty in handling. Another reason may be that to acknowledge before the children that the parents are having difficulty would be an admission of failure. A third reason for trying to hide their difficulties from their children may be the fear of losing the love of their children. I believe each of these approaches, however well-meaning, are serious mistakes.

Troyer is right in stating that it is amazing how well children can handle situations if they know what is happening and have some idea what to expect. Given some time they may adjust to changes even more readily than the parents.[7] Moreover, trying to protect them when they will eventually find out rather suddenly does them more harm than good. Children often like surprises, but never this kind. To hide the problems parents are having in order to avoid the appearance of failure is also a serious mistake. From a Christian perspective, the only adequate basis for enduring husband-wife relationships and enduring parent-child relationships is the mutual acceptance of the Christian doctrine of forgiveness. The doctrine of forgiveness is based on the doctrine of justification by faith. This is the faith to believe that, because of what God has done for us in Jesus Christ, we are called to have the courage to believe that we are forgiven for our mistakes. It requires of us that we not only not hide the fact that we have made mistakes either from ourselves or others but it also requires that we forgive others. We need to accept our need for forgiveness because there are things we have said and done which we cannot undo.

Parents who fear that children will find the truth about their imperfection and vulnerability and will stop loving them have a delightful surprise in store if they will have the courage to confess to their children that they are in some ways failures as parents. They will discover the miracle of love God gives to children. Such a confession will not threaten their relationship with their children. It will strengthen it. Until they are willing to face this reality in the presence of their children, the children are likely to blame themselves. Later, when they are older and develop a more accurate perception of the situation, the damage done to their own emotions may be so serious that their own emotional lives may be very hard to manage.

A final word of caution and some comfort for those parents who do try to protect their children from knowing what is happening are in order. The word of caution is that the couple can overdo the exposure. Verbal fighting in the presence of children can inflict great damage on the children. The preparation of the children should be done calmly with the parents together. The word of comfort, therefore, is that those parents who have protected their children from some of the family quarrels are not all wrong. Some protection is needed; but when it is overdone, it is more harmful than telling the children the truth. By telling them the truth calmly, we not only help them bear it better but also we contribute to their development of respect for integrity.

Letting the Children Love Both Parents

It is also important to the emotional well-being of the children to give them freedom to continue to love both parents after the divorce. This means that each parent must avoid the temptation to get back at the other parent indirectly through the children by saying ugly things about the other parent. This practice may be interpreted by the children as a way of saying to them something like this: if you expect to continue to receive my love, you must not love your other parent. Children should not be put under pressure to make such a choice. No matter how unworthy the other parent may be as a parent, the children are likely to continue their love. To be forbidden such will create serious conflicts in their emotions. Part of the process of healing that needs to occur between the husband and wife is, therefore, very important to the fostering of healthy relationships between the children and their parents and to their own emotional lives as parents as well. It is that the parents should allow the hostility they had toward each other to die. In order to have good relationships with their children, they need to come to a mutual acceptance of each other. Julie List, in *The Day the Loving Stopped*, says parents should never malign each other before the children.[8] When parents have learned these lessons, it will be much easier for them to accept the right and the need of the children to love both parents. By so doing also, they will make an important contribution to the emotional adjustment of the children.

Continued Acceptance of Parental Responsibility

Parents who are divorced need to remember that they are still parents and that, while some of their rights and privileges as husband and wife have been taken away or given away, they still have most of them as parents despite some modifications that have been required by the new situation. Among other things, this means that for the emotional security of the children there are still some decisions the parents should make for the children. While the laws regarding the freedom of the children to make some decisions on their own, depending on their ages, vary from state to state, it creates a terrible burden on the children to have to make them.[9] It is often unfair to them, for example, to ask the children to decide where they will spend Christmas, how long they want to stay with which parent, or with which parent they would prefer to live. While there are exceptions, in most instances it would be far better if the parents would agree privately what would be better for the children and quietly announce it to the children. They should not put the necessity of choosing between them on the children. There may be cases where they agree to allow the children to make choices that do not involve choosing between them.

However, there is danger in allowing too much freedom of choice even in those areas that do not involve choosing between parents. The moral as well as the emotional well-being of children is at stake here. Too much freedom for the children of divorce can have the same effect on them that it often has among the children of those who are still married. The children may conclude that the parents do not care what they do; since they do not care what they do, in fact, they do not care about them at all. Choices the children can handle are all right to be allowed, but in my opinion, most children in our society are given too many free choices before they are morally and emotionally mature enough to handle them. This problem seems especially prominent among the children of the divorced. Some freedom and responsibility is good for the children of course, and in some instances new responsibilities given to the children of divorce can help them to grow up to handle responsibility well. Let divorcees beware of failing to continue to accept their own responsibilities as parents. Those who neglect these responsibilities are, in the long run, inviting heartbreak for themselves and blighting the growth and development of their children.

Introducing Prospective New Mates

One of the most devastating experiences of the children of the newly divorced is the discovery that one of their parents has a new friend of the opposite sex. While the discovery of new companions is often desirable and inevitable, for the sake of the children, Julie List says that it is not wise to introduce the children to a new boyfriend or girl friend too soon. One problem she notes is that children may form attachments quickly and that if there are several friends in succession having to make and break several new attachments creates an unbearable burden for the children. She recommends that a parent not introduce the children to a prospective new mate unless the parent is fairly certain of the permanency of the relationship.[10] I would add that the introduction of a new female friend by the father immediately after the divorce, for example, may also tempt the children to believe they have been betrayed.

I have argued earlier that entering new relationships with the opposite sex too soon can be bad for the husband or wife. It can also be bad for the children. It would probably be better for the children, in most instances, if they are given some time between relatedness to their former parents and relatedness to any newcomers into the family picture. It would also be helpful if before the introduction of a new prospective partner, the children can be given some preparation. Do not spring the new partner on them suddenly. Give them time to think about it, and recognize with them that you understand that no one can replace their original parents and that they are not expected to stop loving the absent parent.

Parents should recognize that the introduction of a new prospective mate can offer promise or threat to the emotional well-being of the children. If the transition from one marriage to another is handled properly by the divorced parents and the new parent, the children will usually make the adjustment. It is important that the new mate and parent figure coming into the picture be patient and give the children some time to make the transition. For the success of the transition, moreover, the mutual understanding and cooperation of both the other parent and the new parent is absolutely necessary. Sometimes that new parent will have to earn the respect of the children, and that may take some time. It may be helpful for the new parent coming into the picture to tell the children how he or she feels about the situation, to tell them plainly that the new parent has no intention of trying to replace the other parent in their love. At the same time, both the parents have to make it clear to the children that there are some roles once filled by the original parent who is absent that must now be filled by the new parent. If the children are given time and understanding and the new parents provide emotional security in a loving environment where the basic needs of the children are met, they will usually adjust.

Consistent Discipline

One of the most confusing and devastating experiences of children is the inconsistency of the discipline of the children by the parents. Differences in discipline between fathers and mothers in marriage vary, but the differences appear to become more acute when the parents are divorced. A recent study published by the National Council of Family Relations provides some information which may be important for divorced parents and from which they can learn. The study indicates that it is very common after the divorce for the father's visits with the children to become less frequent between the second month and the second year of the divorce. Even so, the men suffer from depression, perhaps guilt, and a desire to see their children more often. As a result, when they do get together with their children, because they want their infrequent visits to be happy, they are at first too easygoing. By the end of the second year, however, they begin acting more like fathers, but they still tend to be freer, less affectionate, and less committed to the responsibility for discipline than those fathers in a marriage that is still intact.

In contrast, mothers who still usually receive custody of the children feel the heavy weight of responsibility and often tend to compensate for the absent father's authority by giving too many commands. The child, feeling the weight of the additional pressure, often rebels, and many conflicts between mother and child ensue. By the end of the second year, the mothers settle down and become somewhat less authoritarian and more consistent and successful in their efforts to control the children. In some cases, the results of the extremes and inconsistencies are that the insecurity of the children is greatly increased, and to defend himself (or herself) the child will often pit one parent against the other. The rebelliousness increases along with estrangement from both parents and further heightening of the child's insecurity. The obvious lesson of this study is that parents should take time separately from the child to discuss the problem of discipline calmly and agree on some consistent pattern.[11] As a result, if they follow the pattern on which they agree, the child is more likely to adjust to the situation and experience something nearer to normal growth.

Visitation

One of the most serious problem areas for divorcees and their children is the problem of visitation. Despite the fact that visitation rights are often fixed as a part of the agreement in the divorce and usually approved by both parents, there is often reluctance by one or both partners to allow the visitation required by the agreement. Most children still love both their parents, regardless of what they have done. One of the most impressive examples of this fact is the way a child removed from his parents and placed in a foster home because of child abuse will still cry to see the very parent who was guilty of the abuse. Most of the studies I have read, moreover, indicate that in most cases the children of divorce need regular visits with the absent parent. Fathers are often the worst violators of what is considered proper. The reasons are sometimes understandable, for in some instances still, the father is left with a very difficult economic burden and has very little spare time. More often than not, however, it appears to be a matter of neglecting to do what the father really knows he should. Many fathers underestimate the significance of these visits.

Warner Troyer talked to hundreds of children of divorce about this problem.[12] He says that often the father breaks his promises, keeps his children waiting, and offers a gift to compensate for his guilt. The gifts are all right, but they are little compensation for the self-giving of time and compensation which the children need. Troyer also says parents often err in thinking that the visits always have to include entertainment. Often the most meaningful visits according to the children are times when the parent and child do nothing but get together and talk. It is especially valuable for the absent parent to be present at those events which are important to the child, such as a school play, concert, or athletic event.

It is equally important, however, for the absent parent to make extra phone calls at unexpected times, write brief letters, or drop by for a few minutes between scheduled visits when that is possible and permissible.

Also, it is valuable to establish some continuity between visits by sharing with the children in planned projects where parent and child work together on some project they may continue on the next visit. This helps the parent in the problem of self-discipline in planning and gives the children something to which they may look forward. In addition, it is important when there is more than one child to be visited that time be arranged not only to visit with them together but to spend some time with each child individually as well. As difficult as this may be, the rewards make it worth the price it requires.[13]

It is also important to the success of visitations for the parents to let the visits take place not only with their genuine permission but also in the context of self-control. By accepting the right and the need of the children to visit with the other parent, the parents can make the visitation time happier and more successful for the children and for themselves as well. Unfortunately, the hostility of one or both parents toward the very necessity of visitation can make the visits very difficult for the children, so difficult in some instances that the children themselves call them off.[14] Even so, great damage is done by the parent who prohibits the visits. Still, it must be acknowledged that in some instances greater damage is done by the visits, and the children themselves recognize this fact. Thus, we recognize that there may be exceptions to the rule of regular visitations.

However, while admitting that there are exceptions, I would contend that most of the children of divorce still need contact with both parents on a regular basis. The parents, therefore, who want to contribute to the emotional and spiritual well-being of the children, will do well to make whatever sacrifices that may be necessary to have regular times for visitation. The quality of the visitation, moreover, is as important as the frequency. Regular visits and/or phone calls by the absent parent in which interests are shared and the continuation of love is shown can pay rich dividends for both parent and child.

Role Models

Children of divorce in many cases have lost much of the confidence they had in adults, and one of their needs is to have that confidence restored. One way it can be restored is by the behavior of the parents themselves after the divorce is final. If the parents allow hostility and poor communication to continue to dominate their encounters during visitation with the children or in their separate dialogue with the children, they will hurt the children, rather than help them. It is urgent, therefore, that the parents learn to set good examples of self-control and even friendship both for their own emotional, moral, and spiritual well-being and for the well-being of the children. If the parents have experienced the mutual forgiveness about which I wrote earlier, this self-control and friendship should be easy. I have seen examples which are very impressive. One is a minister whose marriage broke up after his children were grown and married. Both parents have grown from the experience, have great respect for each other, and are good friends, despite the fact that they are not likely to remarry. Their friendship has made the adjustment much easier for the children.[15]

It is equally important for the children of divorce to be exposed to families that are still intact and where loving relationships still are dominant. Three sets of circumstances unfortunately often circumvent this need. The first is that often families that are still intact tend to shut their divorced friends and their children out of their social groups. The divorcees feel the pain of this exclusion keenly, and the children suffer from it. Many divorcees have told me they feel rejected by many former friends because they no longer receive social invitations from them. The fact that these exclusions may not be intended to hurt does not remove the fact that they do hurt both the divorcee and the children.

The second set of circumstances often results from the exclusion of divorcees from circles of families that are still intact. It is that sometimes divorcees and their families get together with other divorcees and their children. The resulting environment is not always the best simply because many divorcees have not grown from their experiences. A third set of circumstances may result from contact between the divorcee and the children and families that are still intact. Troyer points out that often families that are intact will avoid demonstrations of affection, loving relationships, and happiness in the presence of the children of divorce because somehow they fear it might make the children feel bad, seeing what they are missing. These families are trying to be kind, but Troyer is probably right in observing that children need to see examples of healthy, happy family life because from them they may learn that not all marriages are doomed to failure.

The church and its organizations is an excellent place where good family models can be observed by the children. Thus, despite the problems some churches have in accepting divorcees, many churches will accept them, and the children need these role models so badly that the divorcees should take their children to church for their sake regardless of the attitude that some members may have toward the divorcees themselves.

The families of the church can be of great help to the children of divorcees simply by accepting these children and by being themselves. Many divorcees' children have been greatly blessed by the ministry of the church. The children of divorcees often recognize this need before the parents do. A wife whose marriage was in trouble confided in me that her own thirteen-year-old son had told his parents they needed to get back to church. They did, and involvement in the church, while it is not a cure-all, contributed to the healing of some of his wounds and those of the marriage. The marriage is still intact. The children of divorce need the church. They will see good role models elsewhere, but in my judgment the average is higher in the church.

Growth

One of the most effective ways parents can contribute to the emotional adjustment and growth of the children is by their own growth. Parents who grow and learn to take good care of themselves are more likely to take good care of the children. It is important not only to set a good example of personal growth before the children but to guide the growth of the children as well. To achieve this dual goal it is important to establish a balance between the dependence, interdependence, and the independence of the parents in relation to the children. This point is important for both parents, but it is especially important for the parent with whom the children are living.

One of the hazards that may threaten the growth of the parent and the children is the temptation of the parent with whom the children live to center all his or her attention on the children and become utterly dependent on the children for emotional strength. The danger is that the children might become so emotionally dependent on the parent that the freedom and independence necessary to maturity are difficult to achieve. It also happens that the parents center so much attention on the children that their own self-identities become tied up with that of the children. Thus, when the children grow and establish those friendships and interests outside the immediate family that gradually lead to independence, the parents may be tempted to resent that movement to freedom and try to prevent it. In so doing they hamper their own growth as well as the growth of the children.

Divorcees need to recognize that the children are likely to grow up and leave them. Those parents, therefore, who become preoccupied with escaping their loneliness by giving all their time to their children may, in some instances, be doing themselves and their children a disservice. They will be wiser and more successful parents if they grow and help the children to grow, fully aware and accepting of the fact that they and the children will eventually have to make their way. Those divorced parents who overprotect their children because they have been hurt are making them more vulnerable to future problems.

Providing a Better Environment

One of the prime concerns of divorced parents should be not so much to win their own way in the battle for child custody as to provide the best environment for the emotional security, adjustment, and growth of the children. Many divorcees will have concluded that the continuation of the marriage is not the best environment for the children. During the divorce proceedings, each parent may be tempted to think the child would be better off with him or her. In the past the awarding of the custody of the child was almost always given to the mother. That is still the most common solution to the problem of child custody, but it is less common now than it was a few years ago. The movie *Kramer vs. Kramer* emphasizes that fact. If the divorced parents want to consider the well-being of the child, they will ask what the best environment for the child might be, considering the circumstances of each parent separately. Sometimes the work schedule and place of the father or the mother may give some clue as to where the best environment might be. In other cases, the home and community setting might indicate what might be the best environment for the child. In still other cases, the emotional makeup of the parents might provide a clue as to what might be the best environment. The most effective divorced parents will be those who learn to assess the question objectively as to the kind of environment that will be best for the children.

Exercising responsibility for the total environment of the children is sometimes a difficult task. For the parent who has custody of the children, this responsibility is particularly important. It seems to be still the case that more often than not the responsibility and right of custody of the children is given to the mother. Often the mother has to work. For those working parents who have to make arrangements for the care of the children while they are working, there are several important details to be considered.

The first is the choice of a day-care facility for small children. Many states now license such facilities, and, where that is the case, it is important to know that the agency used has a license. However, having the proper license is not enough. The kind of persons who work in day-care centers is very important. It is advisable to get acquainted with them and inquire of others who leave children with them about their evaluation of their work. Also, check the facilities for safety hazards. This point is particularly important where the agency is not licensed, but even licensing is not always a guarantee of safety.

Divorced parents do well to leave their children in the very best environment they can afford. It is particularly hazardous for children to be left alone for long periods of time while the custodial parent is working. Such children are too vulnerable to pressures by other unsupervised children and accidents. To be left alone with no supervision for long periods is more responsibility than most children are able to bear. Those who care for your children while you are working should be responsible and loving persons who are in reasonably good health, and ideally with some knowledge of good principles of child care. The best environment also will include opportunities for the children to learn and not simply be "kept." Parents, you do well to investigate every facility and possibility in the community to discover the best care that your children can receive because your well-being, the well-being of your children, and the well-being of society depends on it.

Finally, you are part of your children's environment. You do well to spend as much time with them as you can to meet their basic needs. However, the quality of the time with the children is quite as important as the quantity.

Notes

1. "Violence Against Children," *Encyclopedia Year Book,* 1982, p. 623.
2. David Goodman, *A Parents' Guide to the Emotional Needs of Children* (New York: Hawthorn Books, 1969).
3. Julie List, *The Day the Loving Stopped* (New York: Seaview Books, 1980), p. 178.
4. Ibid., pp. 186, 196.
5. Judith S. Wallerstein and Joan B. Kelly, *Surviving the Breakup: How Children and Parents Actually Cope with Divorce* (New York: Basic Books, 1980).

6. Warner Troyer, "Children of Divorce Speak Out," *Families,* May, 1981, pp. 73-77.

7. Ibid.

8. Jane Lee White, *Sentinel Star,* March 26, 1980, p. 2b.

9. List.

10. Ibid.

11. Shirley Sloan Fader, "How Divorced Parents Bring Up Their Children," *Family Weekly,* March 7, 1980.

12. "Divorced Kids," *Families,* May 1981, pp. 76-77.

13. Ibid.

14. Marilyn Murray Willison, "Children of Divorce," *Family Weekly,* March 12, 1980.

15. Troyer, p. 77.

9
Conclusion: Suggestions for a Creative Response to a Tragedy

Most of what has been written in the preceding chapters has been based on several broad assumptions which are fundamental to me because of my commitment to what I understand to be the requirements of Christian ethics. For those who share my commitment to the ethical teachings of the Bible, I wish in this chapter to restate these general convictions along with a summary of the practical suggestions which seem to me to grow out of them. These practical suggestions have part of their roots in the central ethical teachings of the Bible, as seen through the eyes of Jesus Christ as I understand him, and part of their roots in the practical realities in the world to which these teachings must be related. The suggestions which are summarized should be regarded only as suggestions of possibilities. Each person must decide how the ethical teachings of Jesus can and must be applied in each particular situation.

The first assumption on which all that I have written is based is that we are responsible to God for all our attitudes and actions in relation to others. For those of us who are committed to the lordship of Jesus Christ, our responsibility to him must take first place in our lives. However, our responsibility to God and our responsibilities to our fellow human beings, including our families, can never be completely separated. In the midst of the complexities of human problems, we have to find ways of preserving both our responsibility to God and our responsibility to our fellow human beings.

The second assumption that underlies all that I have written is closely related to the first. A prime ethical principle to be preserved in making a number of decisions that arise in the process of considering a divorce is concern for persons. Those deciding to get a divorce should consider every decision in terms of its effects on all the persons involved in the process.

128

Those persons involved include one's spouse, the children, and often the parents and grandparents as well. Especially important, of course, are one's spouse and the children who are always to be regarded as persons for whom Christ died.

A third assumption which has guided my writing in this book is that the biblical ideal for marriage is a permanent commitment by one man and one woman to each other with no room for divorce for any reason. In marriage problems as in economic, political, and military problems, among others, we are always in danger of losing sight of the radical demands of Christian ethics. The complexities of our lives and our own sin make some compromises almost inevitable in every area of our lives, but we should never take these compromises lightly and rationalize them in such a way as to make them appear to us and to others as absolutely correct. This error is common among those who defend situation ethics.

The fourth assumption that is fundamental to this grows out of the previous one: forgiveness is a central part of the Christian life. The Christian doctrine of forgiveness is assumed to mean that in Jesus Christ we receive forgiveness for all our sins, in marriage as in every other area of our lives. It is assumed also to mean that in experiencing forgiveness we are set free for a new start in marriage as in every other venture in life. It also requires that we never take forgiveness lightly. If we take forgiveness seriously, we must forgive others and seek their forgiveness, but never to sin deliberately, presuming on forgiveness to be received in the future.

The suggestions made throughout the book are profoundly related to these assumptions, and it may be helpful to summarize their meaning as it related to the argument in each chapter.

First, I suggest that both divorcees and those who are concerned about the divorce rate need to see the problem of divorce in a new way and avoid the broad generalizations about the problem that are not only offensive but also inappropriate when applied to individual persons. As I have tried to show, not all the reasons for divorce are bad when the whole context is considered. Those who are concerned about ministry to individuals would do well, therefore, to avoid loud lamentations about the high divorce rate.

Second, I suggest that those who interpret the biblical teaching on divorce recognize that the biblical writers were as seriously concerned with the individual involved in a broken marriage as they were concerned with protecting the sanctity of the marriage covenant. We need to remember that the prime focus of Jesus was on bringing to an end the ancient custom of men treating women as objects. Jesus sought, like the writers of the law in the Old Testament, to restore both man and woman to the dignity, freedom, and responsibility they enjoyed in the creation. To become unduly legalistic, as many do today in condemning divorcees to a life of celibacy, is out of character with the spirit of Jesus and the biblical stress on the family and on Christian freedom.

Third, I suggest that divorcees and others recognize that very often today married persons find themselves in situations where the continuation of marriage is unbearable for the persons involved, so unbearable indeed that continuation would be more destructive on the partners and the children than the breakup of the marriage. If, after either or both partners seek counsel and are unable to save the marriage, then the minister, other church leaders, and friends should do what they can to help the family members make the necessary transition to a new life. By all means they should reassure the couple and the children of their continued love and concern for their total well-being.

Fourth, when married persons find it necessary to break up their marriage, they should give themselves plenty of time to make the adjustments and plans that are required. They should not hesitate to seek whatever counsel is needed from those most qualified to give it. All of us need the help of others. There is nothing disgraceful about asking for that help. Friends of divorcees should respect the right of divorced persons to some privacy, but they should tactfully make clear their availability to the divorcee to help in constructive ways.

Fifth, the divorcee needs to recognize that the loneliness which follows a divorce is a potential hazard, but can be used creatively. Friends of the divorcee cannot expect to get rid of this loneliness, but they can help to make it more bearable, and they should do so in whatever constructive ways that are possible.

Finally, I suggest that the question of remarriage, like the question of marriage in the first place, is a question that each person must decide. Those who are committed to the Christian ethic must remember, however, that it is a decision that should be made in the light of their Christian calling and in the light of the effects a new marriage might have not only on their Christian commitment but also on the children involved. Marriage failure, like other failures in life, can result in growth for those who have the capacity to learn from mistakes. For Christians, growth in obedience to the will of God is the highest good, both for the married and the unmarried.

Appendix A
Understanding the Rise and Fall
of the Divorce Rate

While in college in the late 1940s, in the years following World War II, I remember reading the lamentations and dire predictions about the future of the family in America given out by ministers and marriage and family counselors as they viewed with alarm the rising divorce rate. They were further alarmed by not only the continuation but also the gradual increase of the number of women in the marketplace in the years which followed. Some even predicted that things would get worse. After reaching a peak of 526,000 in 1946, however, the divorce rate gradually declined for several years. Few of the dire consequences anticipated actually materialized in the fifties. In fact, the decade of the fifties is now viewed in retrospect as almost an ideal time when home and family life was healthy and happy and everyone worked together to achieve the prosperity widely enjoyed.[1]

In 1981, however, new cries of alarm were being sounded. In his survey of the seventies Andrew Hacker, professor of political science at Queens College, saw the rising divorce rate and the instability of the family as one of the signs of the malaise of our age.[2] After declining for several years during most of the 1950s, the divorce rate began to rise slowly by the end of the decade and continued to rise throughout the sixties. During the seventies the divorce rate went to an all-time high, over the million mark for the first time, reflecting a phenomenal 75 percent increase in ten years. In the last two decades, it has almost tripled, according to the National Center for Health Statistics.[3] At the same time, the marriage rate declined for several years during the seventies. That fact, along with the rising divorce rate, has increased the number of single adults in our society. The number of singles appears to continue rising, moreover, despite the fact that most divorcees remarry.

How do we explain the rise, the decline, and the new rise in the divorce

132

rate that have occurred in the last thirty-five years? What moral judgment shall we place on the causes? What can we expect in the future? Finally, what can those of us who believe in the importance of conserving stable families do to stabilize family life in the eighties and, at the same time, give assistance to those who suffer because of the changes in the family system? While I am interested in all these questions, the prime concern in this chapter will be to analyze the changes in the divorce rate in recent years.

Some understanding of these changes should be useful for several groups. First, it should be useful to the millions of divorcees in our society because they may have at least a partial basis for increasing their self-understanding. Second, some explanation of the factors in the changing divorce rate should be of help to those who often pass hasty judgment on the divorcees. I refer here to ministers, other church leaders, neighbors, and friends. Finally, and closely related, it should be of help to those who give counsel to divorcees: ministers, psychiatrists, and social workers who deal often with individuals, but do not have the time to study those social factors which contribute to the problems of these individuals.

I am concerned that what follows communicate compassion for the divorcees, but at the same time be objective descriptions of those factors, both personal and social, which appear to explain the rise in the divorce rate during the decade of the seventies. Because of the complexity of forces which converge in bringing about a divorce, it is impossible to be sure you have explained satisfactorily what happens. Statistical analyses are of value, but they cannot tell the whole story. Therefore, what follows should be understood as the modest efforts of one person to explain a very difficult social phenomenon. The explanation will be subject to further reflection and revision.

Before we attempt an analysis of some of the factors, we need to take note of the geographical distribution of the divorce rate. In 1969 the South had the largest number of divorces, with 439,000. In the North Central states, there were 293,000; in the West, 272,000; and in the Northeast, 177,000. However, the West had the highest divorce *rate*, with 6.6 per 1,000 population. This compares with 6.1 per 1,000 in the South. Those states which granted the largest number of divorces in 1979 were California with 137,683, Texas with 92,399, Florida with 69,707, New York with 64,420, and Ohio with 59,548. The following paragraphs will describe some social factors for the changes in the divorce rate in the past three decades.

Changing Tensions in Society

The divorce rate appears to have reached a low during World War II because families were often drawn closer together, despite the frequent paradox of separation. However, immediately following the war, a rapid rise occurred. Two factors may have affected the rise. First, the tensions which had been developing among wartime marriages continued to increase until eruptions occurring after the war brought many marriages to an end. Second, at first after the war there was a period of adjustment when many of the wives who began working outside the home during the war became dissatisfied resuming a role as homemaker and wife. For a few years before many families learned to cooperate in dealing with home chores, many homes were broken. Even so, it appears that, at least compared to the seventies, in the decade of the fifties marriage and family life in the United States were comparatively stable.

However, in the later years of the fifties and the early sixties, vast changes and unrest in society came to be reflected in the breakup of marriages. According to some social analysts, the rise of juvenile delinquency and crime was at least in part related to the growing instability of both society and marriage. Indeed, it seems appropriate to relate the stresses and strains on marriage and the family to the increasing demands of modern society on personality in general.

There are several factors in society which may well have affected the traditional stability of marriage and the family. First among these factors is the increasing economic stress which is aggravated by the rise of inflation during the last few years. Many marital conflicts arise in conflict over money matters. Robert Weiss, for example, suggests that socioeconomic factors are among the major factors in marital separations. He focuses on the interest of those who break up the marriage in improving their economic status and in developing their personal possibilities at the same time.[4] A second factor is the uncertainty of world conditions and the continual threat of war. It may well be that the *threat* of war and the uncertainties associated with it may create more stress in the family than the certainty of war when it is in process. That many today take the constant threat of war seriously is beyond doubt. The day I wrote these lines, for example, the morning newspaper reported a recent Gallup poll as indicating the 47 percent of those surveyed believe that we will be involved in a nuclear war in ten years. A third factor in the tense atmosphere of our time is the moral revolution which has not only brought about a significant increase in moral relativism but also widespread confusion over moral values. Moral conflict is widespread. Moral libertinism has been paralleled by such guilt as to produce a backlash and a return to a more conservative morality. *Time* magazine reported recently that there may be a moral counterrevolution in process.[5] The basis of this suggestion is a survey by Yankelovich which suggests that, despite the moral revolution, a majority of Americans still hold to values and ideas about marriage and the family that could still be properly described as conservative. Moreover, many who had embraced the moral revolt are now returning to more conservative views because they did not find their moral libertinism at all satisfying.

Some are caught in the middle and honestly do not know how to make a moral decision. Thus, conflict often develops between parents who are committed to one set of values and their children who are being exposed in society to another set of values. It is a tough time to be married and a tougher time to rear children. This fact and the tensions in society may be reflected in three closely related recent developments which are important to an understanding of the family situation. The first of these developments is the increase in the number of singles in our society. The second is the increase in the number of persons who are getting married later in life. The third is the increasing number of couples who choose not to have children or who decide to have fewer children than their counterparts twenty years earlier.

Peer Pressure

A second factor in the rising divorce rate may be the increase among young couples of the power of peer pressure. It is easy to establish the fact that peer pressure among college students is the major obstacle to being moral according to their own understanding. That is at least what most of the students I have surveyed say. Among young adults divorce has become the style. In society, generally, it has become accepted. For example, only a few years ago, it would have been very difficult for a divorced person to get elected to a high political office, such as the presidency. In the election of President Reagan, however, his former marriage and divorce were never seriously questioned by any significantly large group so far as I am aware. Not even the ultraconservative groups, such as the Moral Majority, raised the issue as a reason to oppose him. On the contrary, they were very enthusiastic in their efforts to secure his election. I do not intend to imply that conservative groups, such as the Moral Majority, take divorce lightly. It is more likely that they simply overlooked it because they were preoccupied with other issues. Nor am I claiming that peer pressure directly increases the divorce rate.

More likely, peer pressure to do other things increases the stress level in marriage and thus indirectly contributes to the likelihood of divorce. The economic pressure to "keep up with the Joneses," for example, appears to be a very powerful factor. I have been greatly impressed in recent years with the number of instances where a broken marriage was one of the calamities paralleling the rise to economic success in various professions. The competition created among peers in business and the professions, including the ministry, is often devastating to family relations. The attractive, young wife of a very successful friend said to me several years ago: "What good is money and success when there is no love and no time to be together?" The point is that, in the pressure to get ahead today, many neglect other needs of the family.

There is another kind of peer pressure which is more subtle in character. It is the pressure which sometimes arises between friends who are having difficulty in their marriages who tend to aggravate the difficulties others are having, rather than seeking creative solutions. In the process of sharing the miseries of what appears to be a bad marriage, many individuals create a peer pressure which magnifies the problems rather than *seeking answers*.

A final kind a peer pressure which may destroy marriages today is the pressure to develop a sense of identity. Marriage often does create an identity crisis. The process by which two become one, while retaining some genuine individuality is often not well understood. The notion is widespread that self-identity is somehow tied up with career achievement, and it is quite easy for one who has not distinguished himself or herself in a career to begin to wonder after a few years what or who is to blame for what may be considered failure. Often one's mate turns out to be the object of blame and the marriage breaks up.

Often also people marry before a mature sense of self-identity is developed, but while it is in process of development. The marriage then may, and often does, arrest the development process. After the honeymoon wears off, the early preoccupation with childbearing is over, and social involvements, often including those events related to child-rearing are renewed, so also does the quest and the pressure to develop a sense of self-identity. At several stages in family life, the pressure to accomplish something significant outside the home can become a problem to the marriage, especially where there is not open communication and common understanding between married partners.

Narcissism in Society

Inseparable from peer pressure, but distinct enough to be mentioned separately, is a widespread phenomenon in our society which may be called narcissism or me-ism or preoccupation with self. In short, it seems to be the style to be self-centered today. Of course, it is not a new style. The ancient Greeks knew it and immortalized it in the myth of Narcissus, who fell in love with his own image in the waters of a spring and pined away and killed himself. The flower that bears his name is said to have sprung up from the spot where he died. The element of narcissism as self-centeredness in society has been dramatically described in one way by Christopher Lasch in his book, *The Culture of Narcissism*.

It is described in another way by Daniel Yankelovich who says that, according to surveys he did, in the decade of the 1970s many Americans were dominated by an ethic of self-satisfaction, and the old rules of self-denial and self-giving were placed on a back burner.[6] Fortunately, however, before the decade was over, it was becoming obvious that the egotistical ethic did not work well. According to Yankelovich, being a slave to desire is self-destructive. It is also destructive of family relationships; when two people in the intimacy of family relationships are both bent on satisfying their own desires with no thought of sharing, giving, or community, trouble is almost certain to come. Thus, it appears to me that such self-centeredness which Yankelovich says dominated the 1970s may well have contributed to the rise of the divorce level to the one million mark, and the divorce rate to 50 per 100 marriages between 1975 and 1977. It appears that for some at least there was a confusion between their desire for self-identity and their self-centeredness. They thought that breaking loose to give full expression to their own desires would turn out to be a creative experience, leading to self-discovery and creativity. For some, divorce seemed to be a necessary stage in this quest. But Yankelovich says that for those dominated by self-centeredness, the result they hoped for did not materialize. Self-centeredness is, in short, destructive of both the self and of marital relationships.

Women's Liberation

While self-centeredness as a popular ethical philosophy may have made its contribution to the growth of women's liberation, a more profound and valid source of inspiration for the women's liberation movement has been the growth of interest in human rights, especially interest in justice and equality for minority groups. While the connection between the rise of women's liberation and the rising divorce rate in the 1970s is not easy to prove, there is likely some relationship. There seems to be for many couples a gap in the understanding of their relationships which may have been widened by the women's liberation movement. The rise in the divorce rate may mean in part that the only way some women could achieve equality in marriage was to get out of the marriages they were in. The high rate of remarriage among the newly divorced in the last decade may reflect a desire to find a marriage partner who was open to equality. Still others preferred to find equality in the job market where, at least in some cases, the law was on their side.

The conflict in the expectations of marital responsibilities and privileges is very old and is well documented by Elaine Tyler May as an old problem.[7] She points out, moreover, that one of the earliest explanations of the rising divorce rate was given in 1897 by Columbia law professor Walter Wilcox, who argued that the emancipation of women was the major cause for the high divorce rate. For him it was a tragic shame. However, for James Lichtenberger at the University of Pennsylvania, what Wilcox regarded as a tragedy, was rather a reason to celebrate because of the new opportunities open to women.[8] To Lichtenberger, therefore, the rise in the divorce reflected the advance of women toward freedom as persons. Today the same viewpoint is reflected in the thinking of many feminist leaders and others.

However, despite the fact that Elaine May claims the most common explanation of the rising divorce rate is the rise of concern for women's rights, it seems unclear how the two are related. To cite women's liberation as the main reason for the rising divorce is too simple.[9] One could argue that if the women's rights were the main factor in the rise of the divorce rate, then in recent years when they came to enjoy far more rights and privileges in the social and economic system than ever before, the divorce rate should have declined in the last decade. In fact, as we have shown, it has continued to climb. Of course, feminist leaders could point out that women still have a long way to go before they achieve full equality with men. In summary, though we cannot prove the connection conclusively, it seems that women's liberation and conflicting expectations between women and men in marriage have been among the significant factors in the rise of the divorce rate.

Personal Factors

Concentration in these pages has been on the social factors that may have some bearing on the rising divorce. Virtually nothing has been said about the personal factors or personal explanations given by the divorcees themselves. Throughout most of the early history of our country, the most common single explanation of the rising divorce rate in our country was a personal explanation. The cause was said to be personal depravity. Despite the fact that social analysts were beginning to place the blame on social forces, especially in the cities before 1900, individuals seeking divorces and many moralists saw personal factors as fundamental causes of the rising divorce rate. At this point it is necessary to acknowledge some uncertainty as to the identity of personal and legal factors, but we have been unable to find adequate means of distinguishing them. Although we rely mainly on the personal causes as reported in the legal records, we must recognize that they may not reflect precise accuracy in explaining even the personal causes. However, they may be regarded as having general validity because among the legal grounds for allowing divorce, the ones we shall mention are those chosen by the divorcees as coming the nearest to explaining their particular problem.

Desertion

In 1867 desertion was listed as the largest single cause of divorce, with 41 percent listing it as the main ground. The social circumstances which may explain the prevalence of this cause are easy to discern. They include the widespread disillusionment and moral chaos following the Civil War, as well as the desperate economic problems which emerged not only in the South but also in the North. By 1948, however, desertion had moved to second place, and at 17.8 percent was actually a relatively small minority in the nation as a whole. In a few states, nonetheless, it was still listed as the major cause. These states included New Jersey, Illinois, Delaware, Maryland, District of Columbia, and Virginia. It seems worthy of note that each of these states where desertion was still the major reason given have heavily industrialized and urban areas. The absence of New York State from this list is due to the fact that there was no law allowing divorce on grounds of desertion. Here we may well see the overlapping of social and personal factors in the divorce rate. Economic stress in modern industrialized society may place a very heavy strain on personal relationships in marriage, and the frustration among many males over being unable to live up to their own economic expectation may have led them to desert their families. The assumption that in 1948 most of the deserters were male is based on the fact that, at that time in all the states, most of the divorces were granted to wives.[10]

Cruelty

Cruelty, which was regarded as a minority among the causes of divorce in 1867, has gained ground steadily for the last one hundred years. In 1948 it was listed as the major cause in the nation as a whole. The language of the laws allowing cruelty as a ground for divorce vary widely from state to state, which suggests that the stated cause of cruelty may reflect a wider variety of factors than the word *cruelty* may suggest. The various laws recognize mental and physical cruelty, as defined in a variety of ways. Despite its prominence and variety as a leading cause, it appears that as a personal cause it presents only a surface explanation which may be symptomatic of a variety of deeper causes, which overlap with other causes.

Adultery

Adultery was a major cause in 1867 with 33 percent listing it as the reason for divorce. While it is now widely recognized as justifiable grounds for divorce, it is now listed very rarely as a major legal cause of divorce. In most areas it is listed as the cause of the very small minority of cases. The state of New York is the notable exception. Adultery was still the second leading cause of divorce until the mid 1800s and has declined steadily ever since. In 1948 it was listed as the cause in only 4.5 percent of the divorces in the United States. It would probably be a mistake, however, to conclude that adultery is less common now than it was in the nineteenth century. On the contrary, recent studies indicate that it is now more profoundly related to the first two causes.

Other Causes

In addition to the causes mentioned already, drunkenness, failure to provide, and a combination of other causes are listed by various states, but they appear to play a minor role in most states.

Conclusion

There is value in reflection on the social factors and the legal-personal causes of divorce because they provide some basis for understanding the problem. Individuals with marital problems and counselors would do well to remember that every divorce is a unique experience. It is, therefore, risky to attempt simple social or legal explanations. We must learn to see every divorced person as an individual with problems and possibilities that are different from all others. We can, nevertheless, learn from each other and give support to each other as we seek to understand and appreciate a variety of resources which can sustain us through the common crises of life.

Notes

1. Andrew Hacker, "Survey of the '70s, *1980 Britannica Book of the Year,* p. 129.
2. Ibid.
3. *The Orlando Sentinel Star*, June 9, 1981.
4. Robert Weiss, *Marital Separation* (New York: Basic Books, 1975, Ch. 1).
5. *Time*, November 21, 1977.
6. Daniel Yankelovich, "Are You Taking Risks with Your Life," *Parade*, May 24, 1981.
7. Elaine Tyler May, *Great Expectations: Marriage and Divorce in Post Victorian America* (Chicago: University of Chicago Press, 1980, pp. 1-3).
8. Ibid.
9. Ibid., p. 6
10. Alfred Cahen, *Statistical Analysis of American Divorce* (New York AMS Press, 1968, p. 35).

Appendix B
Divorce in Christian History

In addition to applying our understanding of the teachings of the Old Testament and the New Testament to the problem of divorce and remarriage today, it might be helpful to review the way the church has understood and applied the biblical teaching to the divorce and remarriage question throughout the centuries of Western Christian history. This review is important because the variety of views exhibited by the church through the centuries has not only reflected some of the varieties of views in the culture in which the church existed but it has also influenced that culture and the ideas of the church on divorce in the present.

Cultural Diversity

While the church has not reflected all of the views of divorce that have been common in the cultures of the ancient past, it has exhibited some of them. In addition, it is unclear to what degree cultural tradition has influenced the ideas of the church on divorce, it seems apparent that it has had some impact on the church. It appears that at least five separate traditions about divorce prevailed in various cultures of the ancient past. The first of these traditions, found in many ancient tribes in America, Africa, and Asia, emphasized a rather lax marriage bond, with the freedom of either partner to dissolve it at their pleasure. With the no-fault divorce laws now common in many states, it appears that our culture is moving rapidly toward this tradition again.

The second ancient tradition, perhaps in some cases a reaction to the lax view, went to the opposite extreme. It stressed the indissolubility of marriage, not allowing divorce or remarriage for any reason. This tradition was not only common among the Papuans of New Guinea and the Veddas of Ceylon but in time it became popular in Christian lands as well.

143

The third tradition allowed divorce on the basis of mutual agreement, except in the case of assault or some other form of serious misconduct. Then the wronged party could get the approval of the tribal chief to divorce even an unwilling marital partner. The Karo-Karo of Sumatra are examples of this tradition.

A fourth tradition gave man alone the decision of divorce. Though there were some exceptions and qualifications here and there, this view seems to have been common in the cultures of the ancient Chinese, the Aztecs, and the cultural context of the ancient Near East out of which the ancient Hebrews emerged. Later the same view emerged in ancient Christianity and still later in ancient Islam.

A final tradition found among some of the early American tribes gave the right of divorce to the woman.

Despite the variety of customs on divorce among the ancient primitive cultures, divorce seems not to have been as common among them as it is today. The laws and customs concerning divorce, moreover, were often closely related to conceptions of freedom in each particular culture.[1]

The First Three Centuries of Christianity: Variety

The views on divorce which eventually won their way in the early church may well have been related to the prevailing tendencies in biblical interpretation which became dominant. These early tendencies were dominated by legalism as the church struggled over questions of: (1) what should be included in the canon, (2) how the literature being approved for inclusion in the New Testament should be interpreted, and (3) how the church could protect itself from the loss of self-identity as something unique in the ancient world. The church tended often to become legalistic in its interpretation of ethics as it had become legalistic in its interpretation of Christian theological thought in general. Thus, just as the early church interpreted many of the sayings of Jesus as recorded in the Gospels as prohibiting war, so it came to interpret this saying as prohibiting divorce. However, the meaning of a variety of passages on the subject of divorce seemed less clear to the church than those relating to war. As a result, there was more discussion and debate on divorce than on war.[2] Gradually, however, in the discussion of the first three centuries the general condemnation of divorce gained ground. By the time of Augustine, separation was considered acceptable, but not remarriage. However, Augustine did insist that the right of separation belonged to the woman as well as the man.

The Emergence of Medieval Views

In his arguments Augustine prepared the way, moreover, for the view of the medieval church on divorce, as he influenced the developing views of the church on other subjects. The Synod of Carthage in AD 407 established the view that was to dominate the church for centuries. Before that time, there was much compromise; but after that, Augustine's view generally prevailed. Even so, the conflict between the strict stand of the church and the culture of some areas still resulted in some compromise. England and Gaul are examples where divorce and remarriage were still sometimes allowed. The solidifying of the strict view was expressed in AD 1164 in Peter Lombard's highly influential *Sentences*, which declared: (1) that the marriage covenant made marriage in fact indissoluble, and (2) that the church alone, and not the marriage partners, could decide on questions of conflict. Thus, the strict stand condemning divorce and remarriage which is dominant in Catholic moral theology today was born.

However, definitions of marriage were soon developed and/or formalized which continued to provide exceptions which really amounted to the toleration of divorce. These exceptions included two specific conditions. The first was the case where a Christian convert was abandoned by a mate who was an infidel. The second was the case where the marriage was never consummated. It appears that even with these exceptions, the possibility of divorce was severely limited. Again, however, the variety of definitions and interpretations which followed, along with the implementation of these interpretations in religious and civil practice, resulted in wide liberty throughout the Middle Ages. This liberty was particularly available to those who could afford to secure the services of high priced church lawyers. Often in the procedure there was fraud and perjury. In short, there were ways of getting around the church laws for those who were wealthy and wise.[3]

Despite the enlargement of definitions of a properly consummated marriage, and therefore affect Roman Catholic Church decisions concerning divorce, the general position of the medieval church on divorce prevails in the Roman Catholic Church today. The net result is that divorce is really discouraged but is nevertheless available. The term generally used to validate the termination of a marriage which includes the permission to remarry is *annulment*. Technically, annulment is not regarded as divorce because in it the marriage is not regarded as a valid marriage.

The Orthodox Church, which resulted from a split between the Eastern and Western church in AD 1054, has no official position on divorce, though it does lay stress on several principles by which decisions are expected to be guided. Generally, divorce is allowed only for adultery; but in practice, other forms of misconduct are defined as the equivalent of adultery. The Orthodox Church also takes the view that for a marriage to be valid, it must have the blessing of the Church; and by this view, it assumes control over the dissolution of marriage as well. In modern practice, the diocesan officials often do no more than confirm or set aside the decision of the civil authorities. In some cases they may counsel or censure the marital partners. In Greece, for example, an attempt at reconciliation by the bishop is required before approval is given to the couple to go through the civil procedure of seeking a divorce.[4]

The Reformation and Emergence of Modern Views

The coming of the Protestant Reformation brought a wider variety of views on divorce and remarriage, and broad generalizations about the Protestant position are not possible. Still, one of the central objections of both Luther and Calvin has been widely influential in many Protestant groups. Both Luther and Calvin challenged the sacramental nature and the indissolubility of marriage. Luther particularly objected to the Roman Church stress on celibacy as a requirement for the clergy and argued that marriage was an institution of this world. Though he had high regard for marriage, he felt that the views of the church were too strict. Luther argued that Roman Church law on celibacy and divorce encouraged vice and discriminated against the poor since the rich who could afford the church lawyers could get annulments. At the same time Luther also was fundamentally opposed to divorce. However, his view of the fall of man as having corrupted marriage as well as other institutions affected significantly the way he interpreted divorce and remarriage. Therefore, though he thought divorce was a sin, he believed that both divorce and remarriage were justified some times as the lesser of two evils.

Luther held three views on remarriage. First, he was very reluctant to justify divorce for one who was a Christian, but he accepted it in case of desertion and adultery. Second, Luther believed that for one who was married to an unbeliever Paul provided grounds for both divorce and remarriage, according to the choice of the individual. Third, because he regarded it as an unanswered question in the gospel, Luther was reluctant to comment on the right of remarriage for the innocent party. The uncertainties in biblical teaching, plus his stress on the involvement of the whole family and society in marriage, were both important problems to Luther. This led to a statement of his view that such matters as divorce and remarriage were not the prerogative of the church to decide, but should rather be decided by the civil government.[5] Luther's personal views later in life seemed almost to justify polygamy as he looked lightly on the marriages of some of the German princes.[6]

Luther's objections led to the development of civil laws and religious practices that relaxed some of the strictness of the church on divorce for all people. Gradually, therefore, in Lutheranism both divorce and remarriage became accepted and written into the laws of many countries where Lutheranism spread during the three centuries following the Reformation.

Similarly, Calvin and his followers soon allowed divorce when serious grounds were found. Despite the apparent legalism in his thought, reflecting his sharp legal mind, Emerson claims that the laws on marriage and remarriage in Geneva which Calvin influenced are not legalistic in their interpretation of biblical teaching on divorce and remarriage. The laws adopted by the Geneva Council in 1561 reflect not only the ideas of Calvin but also the kind of thinking that came to influence much of Europe and England. Calvin's influence on much of England came both indirectly through the model he helped to create in Geneva and through his extensive correspondence with church and political leaders all over Europe. Emerson argues that it was the body of law in Geneva, however, more than the personal views of either Luther or Calvin that marks the transition from regulation of divorce and remarriage from the church to society and civil authority. The laws adopted by the Geneva Council are extensive, complicated, and, in some cases, ambiguous. Despite the ambiguities in the law, however, several things seem clear. First, like Luther, Calvin regarded divorce as wrong, against nature. Second, he recognized it as a reality which in some instances was justified. Third, although Calvin and the laws are unclear on the circumstances justifying remarriage, both allowed it.[7]

The Church of England, despite the well-known story of Henry VIII, who was mainly responsible for the break with Rome because of his own interest in getting a divorce (or annulment), has generally adhered to Roman canon law until the twentieth century, when gradually some reform emerged. It will still not marry a divorced person, but it will give formal blessing to remarriage of divorced persons. Also, the Church of England does not excommunicate persons who get divorced, but they are not allowed to take communion except by special permission of the church. Thus, in England the position of the church on divorce has been more conservative than in mainland Europe. Efforts were made by Edward VI to liberalize divorce laws, but parliament failed to adopt his suggestions. Full divorce at the time was available only by an act of parliament. The best to be gained before 1857 was a church decree of separation from "bed and board," and this was available only for cruelty and adultery.

Divorce in the American Colonies

Despite early dependencies and close relationships between Colonial New England and England, differences between the Puritan and the independent churches in the colonies on the subject of divorce developed early. In contrast to the strict conservative regulations against divorce in England, regulations in the New England colonies were relaxed almost from the beginning.[8] Both divorce and remarriage were allowed for a variety of causes.

In the South, however, not a single example of divorce has been found in five southern provinces before the Revolution.

The Middle Colonies were somewhere between the Northern and

Southern Colonies not only geographically but also in their attitudes and regulations on divorce.

Perhaps the most modern example of divorce legislation in the Colonial period is to be found in Connecticut. Here reasonable grounds for divorce were allowed and husbands and wives were given equal consideration before the law.

The variety of views on divorce and remarriage which developed among various Protestant sects in the Colonial and the post-Revolutionary period has continued to the present. If there is any change in the last twenty-five years, it appears that a more liberal attitude toward divorce and remarriage has become increasingly common. These more liberal views as expressed by various denominational leaders do not reflect any change in their views of the sanctity of marriage however. Most denominational leaders still uphold monogamy and permanency in the husband-wife relationship as the ideal. The changing of their attitudes toward divorce and remarriage is related not to their views of marriage, but to an increasing compassion on the part of church leaders for those individuals who are victims of a bad marriage which apparently has no hope of redemption because it takes two willing partners to redeem a bad marriage.

Thus, it is easy to find a clear paradox among the writings of most denominational leaders on the subject of divorce and remarriage. On the one hand, these leaders often lament the rise of the divorce rate in recent years. On the other hand, they show increasing concern for their responsibility to minister to the needs of the divorcees both as individuals and as parents where there are children involved. This increased concern is evident not only in public and published announcements but also in literature which is directed to helping these new singles with their problems and in retreats where divorcees and other singles are brought together with each other for mutual comfort and instruction from qualified leaders who help them through their pilgrimage.

The variety of views and the increasing concern on the part of the churches to minister to divorced persons will be evident from a brief examination of recent denominational views and positions on divorce and remarriage.

The United Methodist Church

In the late 1950s, the discipline of the Methodist Church did not allow ministers in the Methodist Church to remarry divorced persons whose former mates still lived, except in two cases. First, they were allowed to remarry the divorced couple to each other. Second, they were allowed to marry the innocent party.[9] Compared to other denominational customs at the time, this position was an exceptionally strict one.

However, the 1980 *The Book of Discipline of the United Methodist Church* is an excellent example of the growth of compassion shown for divorcees in recent years. In this volume the official position of the leaders of the United Methodist Church is set forth. This position recognizes that some marriages develop differences between partners that are irreconcilable. Divorce is viewed as a regrettable fact, but the right of divorced persons to remarry is affirmed. Furthermore, the church expresses concern for the well-being of minor children and encourages divorced parents to continue sharing responsibility for them. Finally, the church accepts its responsibility to minister to all the members of divorced families.[10] However, it is important to understand that the *The Book of Discipline* is regarded by the United Methodist Church, as a general, but not absolute guide. It is made clear that it is not to be regarded by all Methodists as sacrosanct. Each General Conference is free to modify or supplement the positions taken here. At the same time, the views set forth in *The Book of Discipline* reflect the views of the many General Conferences that make up the United Methodist Church. Thus, it may be regarded as fairly representative of the views of the United Methodist Church.

Presbyterian Church

The United Presbyterian Church, U.S.A., adapted a statement in 1953 which allowed remarriage after divorce on scriptural grounds, but it did not interpret these scriptural grounds explicitly. It did require a one year waiting period for the divorced party, but where that rule could be shown to the Presbytery by the minister to be satisfied, the minister was free to decide whether to remarry a particular person. In line with the tradition of Calvin, the minister was admonished to be sure of the individual's repentance of sin and a genuine determination to make the next marriage work.[11] The minister was also admonished not to remarry a divorced person from another denomination whose denominational rules forbid remarriage.[12]

In the 120th General Assembly in 1980, the Presbyterian Church in the United States recognized divorce as justifiable on grounds of adultery or where the continuation of the marriage would threaten the well-being of the partners or that of the children. Divorce is a reality which the church must recognize despite the fact that it is a necessity born of sin. The church also recognized its responsibility to minister to the families of all divorced persons including ministers of the church; while the statement does not mention remarriage directly, several sections appear to this writer to assume the freedom of either partner to remarry. This assumption seems to be implied particularly in the statements on the responsibility of the church to be a forgiving and healing force.[13]

The Episcopal Church

In America the Episcopal Church did not recognize divorce until 1973. However, even before 1973 it did provide, somewhat like the Roman Catholic Church, several grounds for annulment, which was a way of declaring that a true marriage had never been achieved. Also before 1973 a bishop might allow a divorced person to remarry under certain conditions. Further, divorced persons could be given communion provided they could get the approval of the bishop by convincing the bishop that they were sincere in their faith, had genuinely repented, and were trying to live a Christian life.[14]

In 1973 in its sixty-fourth general convention, the Episcopal Church of America made significant changes in its traditional stance toward divorce and remarriage. First, it recognized civil divorce as legitimate. Second, it liberalized its own rules for divorce. Third, it liberalized its rules for remarriage. Thus, the Episcopal Church removed from its regulations the threat of excommunication held over those who ignored the church's rules that the right to remarry must be decided by the bishop or that either the groom or the bride be a member of the church in good standing. Before

1973 permission of the bishop was required to remarry and remain in good standing in the church. Now the parish priest may grant the permission, but one of the marriage partners must be a baptized member of the church.[15]

Baptists

Some research indicates that, while many Baptists oppose divorce except in the case of adultery, there is no official Baptist position on divorce and remarriage because of the unique nature of Baptist polity, stressing as it does the autonomy and independence of each local congregation. The nearest thing to an official position on any ethical question for Baptists consists of resolutions adopted at annual Conventions. While resolutions on family life are not uncommon, I found no resolutions among Baptists in recent years on the subject of divorce and remarriage. However, published articles, unpublished sermons, and letters to the editors of Baptist publications in recent years give evidence of changes occurring in Baptist thought about the subjects of divorce and remarriage. Baptists, like others, continue to stress the sanctity of marriage, but in recent years they have been less inclined than before to condemn those who are remarried as living in adultery. Moreover, the Southern Baptist Convention's publishing agencies have produced a great deal of helpful literature which ministers to the needs and problems of divorcees and their families.

Judaism

Following the Old Testament, the Jewish community continues to recognize both divorce and remarriage as justifiable; but it also continues to regard divorce as a tragedy and as a threat to the continuation of the Jewish community. However, Jewish law as interpreted by many rabbis regards the continuation of a home without love and harmony as worse than divorce. Jewish writers have often condemned Christianity for its strict stand against divorce, yet the divorce rate among Jews is generally lower than the divorce rate among Christians. While Jews recognize the legality of a civil divorce, both Conservative and Orthodox Jews require a religious divorce, a *Get*, which is a Jewish declaration that the marriage is terminated. While some exceptions have been made generally in the Jewish community, only a man can seek divorce; but once the man initiates the effort to obtain a divorce, it may be granted by mutual consent. However, efforts are now under way in the Jewish community to have this regulation changed so that women can have equal access with men to the Jewish divorce courts.

Conclusion

I am in fundamental agreement with the conclusions of Emerson when he presents his general critique of denominational history and views on divorce and remarriage. He says they have failed at several points. First, he says they have failed to understand the Christian concept of time *(kairos)*. By this he means that the denominations generally, while they have sought to free themselves from the bondage of legalism, have failed to give adequate attention to the need for readiness (time) for marriage.

Second, he says denominations have also failed to recognize both the uniqueness of each individual and of the corporate involvement of each individual in his society and culture.[16] Third, he writes that church regulations and guidelines have too often been rooted in the reactions of the culture to the views of the church rather than from the concern of the church for the couple involved in divorce. Here he says there is need for greater stress on what he calls realized forgiveness, which he describes as the recognition of the responsibility of the church and society along with the individuals for the failure of a particular marriage.[17]

While numerous denominations have changed their views on the subject of divorce and remarriage and show more compassion now than they did even in the 1940s and 1950s, in general terms, his criticism is still valid.

In my own counseling and conferences with divorcees in the 1970s and 1980s, I have found that many of them are made to feel like second-class citizens in their churches and are uncertain as to how their own ministers feel about remarriage. Thus, the churches need to find new ways to help these persons; and as I have indicated earlier, this book is dedicated to helping the churches to learn better ways of communicating their caring concern, as well as to helping divorcees to endure and build on their experiences.

It also appears clear that throughout much of its history, the church has tended to legalism in its interpretation of the biblical teaching on divorce.

In so doing, the church has often depersonalized those individuals who have been caught in the throes of bad marriages. At the same time, in upholding the sanctity of marriage, the church has reminded all the members of the church of the importance of covenant commitments to God and to each other in the context of marriage as in the other contexts of our lives. It is a sign of hope, however, that however the church may be failing in other ways, it appears to be moving toward giving the kind of care to divorcees as persons which all of us need. Those facing the possibility of divorce do well to reflect not only on the nature of their commitments but, in those cases where those commitments cannot be kept, they should look to the church for the care they need as well.

Notes

1. Article on "Divorce," in *The New Schaff-Herzog Encyclopedia of Religious Knowledge* (New York: Funk and Wagnalls, 1909), Volume III, pp. 452 *ff.*

2. Ibid., p. 4.

3. Ibid.

4. *Encyclopedia Brittannica,* 1965 edition, Volume VII, pp. 513 *ff.*

5. James G. Emerson, Jr., *Divorce, the Church, and Remarriage* (Philadelphia: The Westminster Press, 1961), pp. 105-107.

6. Ibid., p. 105.

7. Ibid., p. 99.

8. Schaff, p. 454.

9. Emerson, p. 119.

10. *The Book of Discipline of the United Methodist Church,* 1980 (United Methodist Publishing House, Nashville, Tennessee), p. 71.

11. Emerson, p. 127 *ff.*

12. Ibid., p. 129.

13. *Minutes of the 120th General Assembly,* part I, *Journal,* Presbyterian Church in the U.S., p. 180 *ff.*

14. Leo Rosten, ed., *Religions of America* (New York: Simon and Schuster, 1975), p. 105.

15. Ibid., p. 105.

16. Emerson, pp. 139-140.

17. Ibid., pp. 142-143.